Rudyard Kipling, William Ernest Henley

A London Garland

Selected from Five Centuries of English Verse

Rudyard Kipling, William Ernest Henley

A London Garland
Selected from Five Centuries of English Verse

ISBN/EAN: 9783337130015

Printed in Europe, USA, Canada, Australia, Japan

Cover: Foto ©Andreas Hilbeck / pixelio.de

More available books at **www.hansebooks.com**

A
LONDON GARLAND
SELECTED FROM FIVE CEN
TURIES OF ENGLISH VERSE
BY W. E. HENLEY WITH PIC
TURES BY MEMBERS OF THE
SOCIETY OF ILLUSTRATORS

MACMILLAN AND COMPANY
LONDON AND NEW YORK
1895

NOTE

HIS is not a full, much less an exhaustive, collection of Lon(verses. It is only a choice for illustration : a choice, too, representative as it appears than it was in the beginning, it was realised what numbers would lend themselves pictorial treatment, and what numbers would not.

Even so, however, 'tis hoped that *A London Garland*, being selec from some five centuries of verse, will be found to example m differences in method and the point of view, which have ruled passed in English Poetry in the long years dividing the London Chaucer's Prentice and Dunbar's panegyric and the London of *Piccac* and *In The Rain*.

The pictorial commentary is no concern of mine, but is wholly t of the Society of Illustrators, at whose request the little which I had to was done.

W. E. H

27th *November* 1895.

The Members of the Society of Illustrators wish to express their
:s to various Authors and Publishers for permission to include
·ight pieces in this volume.

 ONTENTS

HALF-TITLE. Designed by ALFRED PARSONS

FRONTISPIECE. Drawn by F. A. ABBEY

PREFACE

CONTENTS. Etching by R. W. MACBETH, A.R.A.

LIST OF ILLUSTRATIONS

LIST OF ARTISTS

LIST OF AUTHORS

A STORM FIEND. By FREDERICK SANDYS

A LONDON PRENTICE. GEOFFREY CHAUCER
    Illustrated by *Alice B. Woodward*.

IN PRAISE OF LONDON. WILLIAM DUNBAR

WINDSOR CASTLE. HENRY HOWARD, EARL OF SURREY

PROTHALAMION, OR, A SPOUSAL VERSE. EDMUND SPENSER
    Illustrated by *Walter Crane, A.R.W.S.*

WINDSOR FOREST. MICHAEL DRAYTON
    Illustrated by *Enoch Ward*.

WINDSOR TO LONDON THAMES. MICHAEL DRAYTON.
    Illustrated by *W. L. Wyllie, Frank L. Emanuel,* and *Alfred Parsons*.

A WINTER SONG. THOMAS NASHE

SONG: TO CELIA. BEN JONSON
    Illustrated by *H. Johnson*.

IN LONDON WAY. JOSEPH HALL
    Illustrated by *W. L. Wyllie, A.R.A.*

THE MAY-LORD. JOHN FLETCHER

A LONDON GARLAND

	PAGE
ES ON THE TOMBS IN WESTMINSTER. FRANCIS BEAUMONT Illustrated by *E. H. New* and *Joseph Pennell.*	26
RES TO THAMASIS. ROBERT HERRICK Illustrated by *Douglas Macpherson.*	28
LONG VACATION IN LONDON. SIR WILLIAM DAVENANT	30
ALLAD UPON A WEDDING. SIR JOHN SUCKLING Illustrated by *W. S. Stacey.*	35
EN THE ASSAULT WAS INTENDED TO THE CITY. JOHN MILTON Illustrated by *A. J. Finberg* and *E. G. Hill.*	40
ONDON CAVALIER. ALEXANDER BROME Illustrated by *Claude A. Shepperson.*	41
OWN GALLANT. JOHN WILMOT, EARL OF ROCHESTER Illustrated by *Alfred Pearse, F. W. Lawson,* and *H. R. Millar.*	45
ITY SHOWER. JONATHAN SWIFT Illustrated by *Joseph Pennell.*	47
OMAN OF FASHION. THOMAS TICKELL Illustrated by *Chris Hammond* and *F. H. Townsend.*	50
MPTON COURT. ALEXANDER POPE Illustrated by *J. Fulleylove.*	52
HTWALKING. JOHN GAY Illustrated by *J. Finnemore* and *J. R. Way.*	54
LY IN OUR ALLEY. HENRY CAREY Illustrated by *E. J. Sullivan.*	59
JAMES'S CHAPEL. ANONYMOUS Illustrated by *J. Bernard Partridge.*	62
M RICHMOND HILL (1727). JAMES THOMSON Illustrated by *S. Reid.*	64
DON JAUNTS. HENRY FIELDING Illustrated by *G. Grenville Manton.*	69
DON JARS. HENRY FIELDING Illustrated by *Cecil Aldin.*	71
E RED LION, HENLEY. WILLIAM SHENSTONE Illustrated by *J. S. Crompton.*	73
ON A DISTANT PROSPECT OF ETON COLLEGE (1742). THOMAS GRAY Illustrated by *A. R. Quinton.*	74

CONTENTS

STRAWBERRY-HILL, A BALLAD. WILLIAM PULTENEY, EARL OF BATH

A CHAMBER IN GRUB STREET. OLIVER GOLDSMITH
    Illustrated by *W. W. Russell.*

THE CONTRAST. CAPTAIN CHARLES MORRIS

WAPPING OLD STAIRS. CHARLES DIBDIN
    Illustrated by *W. Thomas Smith.*

HOLY THURSDAY. WILLIAM BLAKE
    Illustrated by *F. H. Crawford.*

LONDON FROM SHOOTER'S HILL. GEORGE GORDON BYRON, LORD BYRON

UPON WESTMINSTER BRIDGE. WILLIAM WORDSWORTH
    Illustrated by *Edgar Wilson.*

THE MERMAID TAVERN. JOHN KEATS
    Illustrated by *Robert Burns.*

MOLESEY HURST. JOHN HAMILTON REYNOLDS
    Illustrated by *Frank Dad, Jack B. Yeats,* and *A. S. Hartrick.*

THE BOY AT THE NORE. THOMAS HOOD
    Illustrated by *R. Vicat Cole.*

A BALLAD OF GUY FAWKES. THOMAS HUDSON
    Illustrated by *W. Rainey* and *A. R. Rackham.*

GOOD NIGHT TO THE SEASON. WINTHROP MACKWORTH PRAED
    Illustrated by *Ronald Gray* and *H. Tonks.*

"O that 'twere possible
After long grief and pain." ALFRED TENNYSON
    Illustrated by *Everard Hopkins* and *Fred. T. Jane.*

THE IDLER. ANONYMOUS
    Illustrated by *A. S. Boyd.*

SUMMER IN HYDE PARK. MATTHEW ARNOLD

A COVENT GARDEN PASTORAL. HENRY S. LEIGH

THE BELLS OF ST. MARTIN'S. HENRY S. LEIGH
    Illustrated by *Archie Macgregor.*

THE BURDEN OF NINEVEH. DANTE GABRIEL ROSSETTI
    Illustrated by *Hal Hurst.*

ST. JAMES'S STREET. FREDERICK LOCKER-LAMPSON
    Illustrated by *J. W. T. Manuel.*

PICCADILLY. FREDERICK LOCKER-LAMPSON
    Illustrated by *A. H. Collings, Oscar Eckhardt,* and Sir *J. D. Linton,* P.R.I.

A LONDON GARLAND

	PAGE
)AY AT HAMPSTEAD. JAMES THOMSON	143
Illustrated by *L. Raven Hill* and *Phil May*.	
NDON PLANE-TREE. AMY LEVY	147
Illustrated by *J. Barnard Davis*.	
.EAM. WILLIAM MORRIS	149
Illustrated by *W. Bayes*.	
)ON SNOW. ROBERT BRIDGES	150
IAMES SUBURB. ROBERT BRIDGES	152
,UTUMN IDYLL. AUSTIN DOBSON	154
Illustrated by *G. D. Hammond* and *Fred Pegram*.	
MALTWORM'S MADRIGAL. AUSTIN DOBSON	161
Illustrated by *G. H. Edwards*.	
MY. RUDYARD KIPLING	164
Illustrated by *W. B. Wollen, R.I.*, and *T. S. C. Crowther*.	
ER THE SPEAKER'S GALLERY. WILFRID SCAWEN BLUNT	167
LONDON SEASON. WILFRID SCAWEN BLUNT	168
DWOOD. WILFRID SCAWEN BLUNT	169
\Y AT HAMPTON COURT. WILFRID SCAWEN BLUNT	171
Illustrated by *W. Hatherell, R.I.*	
N OLD CITY CHURCH. J. ASHBY-STERRY	173
Illustrated by *C. E. Mallows* and *R. Strudwick*.	
'HE RAIN. ROSAMOND MARRIOTT-WATSON	175
Illustrated by *Chadwell Smith*.	
DDLE OF THE THAMES. WILLIAM WATSON	178
Illustrated by *A. Hugh Fisher*.	
'OUNTAIN COURT. ARTHUR SYMONS	180
Illustrated by *W. E. Home*.	
)AFER. JOHN DAVIDSON	181
Illustrated by *J. F. Sullivan* and *W. Luker*.	
LADE OF CLEOPATRA'S NEEDLE. ANDREW LANG	184
Illustrated by *W. L. Wyllie, A.R.A.*	
LADE OF SUMMER. ANDREW LANG	187
Illustrated by *Enoch Ward*.	
A DISTANCE. JUSTIN HUNTLY M'CARTHY	189
Illustrated by *Paul Renouard, W. D. Almond*, and *Aubrey Beardsley*.	

CONTENTS

THE LITTLE DANCERS. W. L. BINYON .
    Illustrated by *A. S. Hartrick.*

NOCTURN. W. E. HENLEY .
    Illustrated by *J. M‘Neil Whistler* and *Arthur Tomson.*

IN WESTMINSTER. W. E. HENLEY
    Illustrated by *Joseph Pennell.*

FOG. W. E. HENLEY .
    Illustrated by *Joseph Pennell.*

LIST OF ILLUSTRATIONS

Design for Wrapper for *A London Garland*. Drawn by G. C. HAITÉ.
    Reproduced by Waterlow and Sons, Limited.

Initial Letters. Drawn by ALFRED PARSONS.
    Reproduced by Waterlow and Sons, Limited.

End Papers. Designed by W. GLEESON WHITE.
    Lithographed by Maclagan and Cumming.

Half-Title and Cover. Designed by ALFRED PARSONS, R.I.
    Reproduced by Waterlow and Sons, Limited.

Frontispiece. By EDWIN A. ABBEY
    Reproduced by Waterlow and Sons, Limited.

Contents. Etching by R. W. MACBETH, A.R.A.
    Printed by F. Goulding.

List of Illustrations. Heading designed by R. A. BELL.
    Reproduced by Waterlow and Sons, Limited.

List of Artists. Heading designed by R. A. BELL
    Reproduced by Waterlow and Sons, Limited.

A Storm Fiend From an unpublished drawing by FREDERICK SANDYS
    Reproduced by the Swan Electric Engraving Company.

Ye Olde Blue Boar. Drawn by ALICE B. WOODWARD
    Reproduced by Waterlow and Sons, Limited.

A LONDON GARLAND

	PAGE
e Themmes! runne softly, till I end my Song." Drawn by WALTER CRANE, A.R.W.S.	10
Reproduced by Waterlow and Sons, Limited.	
... wreaths this king of rivers crowns." Drawn by ENOCH WARD	14
Reproduced by Angerer and Göschl.	
in by London leads." Drawn by W. L. WYLLIE, A.R.A.	16
Reproduced by Angerer and Göschl.	
n Court. Drawn by FRANK L. EMANUEL	17
Reproduced by André and Sleigh.	
owded wharfs, and people-pest'red shores." Drawn by ALFRED PARSONS	18
Reproduced by Angerer and Göschl.	
ie, sweet." Drawn by H. JOHNSON	21
Reproduced by Angerer and Göschl.	
ndon way." Etching by W. L. WYLLIE, A.R.A.	To face p. 22
"How many royal bones Sleep within this heap of stones." Drawn by E. H. NEW	25
Reproduced by A. and C. Dawson.	
"An acre sown indeed With the richest, royall'st seed." Drawn by JOSEPH PENNELL.	27
Reproduced by Waterlow and Sons, Limited.	
with boughes and rushes beautifi'd." Drawn by DOUGLAS MACPHERSON	29
Reproduced by A. and C. Dawson.	
per Thames. Etching by Sir FRANCIS SEYMOUR HADEN, P.R.P.E.	To face p. 34
Printed by F. Goulding.	
"Her feet beneath her petticoat, Like little mice, stole in and out." Drawn by W. S. STACEY	37
Reproduced by the Swan Electric Engraving Company.	
lton. Drawn by A. J. FINBERG	40
Reproduced by Angerer and Göschl.	
garden house in Aldersgate Street. Drawn by E. G. HILL	40
Reproduced by the Swan Electric Engraving Company.	
"Come your ways, Bonny boys Of the town." Drawn by CLAUDE A. SHEPPERSON	42
Reproduced by Angerer and Göschl.	
ntly run through the lungs." Drawn by ALFRED PEARSE	44
Reproduced by Walker and Boutall.	
ere is an End of Bully!" Drawn by F. W. LAWSON	45
Reproduced by A. T. Clarke and Company.	
"A brisk Blade of the Town That takes Delight in roaring." Drawn by H. R. MILLAR	46
Reproduced by Angerer and Göschl.	

LIST OF ILLUSTRATIONS

"A City Shower." Drawn by JOSEPH PENNELL.
    Reproduced by the Swan Electric Engraving Company.
    "In Kensington Gardens to stroll up and down,
    You know was the fashion before you left town." Drawn by CHRIS HAMMOND.
    Reproduced by Waterlow and Sons, Limited.
"I mount on my palfrey as gay as a lark." Drawn by F. H. TOWNSEND
    Reproduced by Angerer and Göschl.
Hampton Court. Drawn by J. FULLEYLOVE, R.I.
    Reproduced by Angerer and Göschl.
Hampton Court. Drawn by J. FULLEYLOVE, R.I.
    Reproduced by Angerer and Göschl.
The Long Walk, Hampton Court. Drawn by J. FULLEYLOVE, R.I.
    Reproduced by Angerer and Göschl.
    "Seiz'd by rough hands, he's dragged amid the rout,
    And stretch'd beneath the pump's incessant spout." Drawn by J. FINNEMORE
    Reproduced by Angerer and Göschl.
"Old Clo'." Drawn and Lithographed by J. R. WAY .   *To face p.*
"To walk abroad with Sally." Drawn by E. J. SULLIVAN
    Reproduced by Angerer and Göschl.
St. James's Chapel. Drawn by J. BERNARD PARTRIDGE.
    Reproduced by the Swan Electric Engraving Company.
    "Or ascend,
    While radiant Summer opens all its pride,
    Thy hill, delightful Shene." Drawn by S. REID.
    Reproduced by Angerer and Göschl.
"My dear, the coach is at the door!" Drawn by G. GRENVILLE MANTON
    Reproduced by Angerer and Göschl.
"And *this* dog smarts for what *that* dog hath done." Drawn by CECIL ALDIN
    Reproduced by the Swan Electric Engraving Company.
William Shenstone writing his poem on the window-pane at the Red Lion, Henley. Drawn by J. S. CROMPTON
    Reproduced by Angerer and Göschl.
"A distant prospect of Eton." Drawn by A. R. QUINTON
    "Ye distant spires, ye antique towers,
    That crown the watery glade."
    Reproduced by Angerer and Göschl.
A Chamber in Grub Street. Drawn by W. W. RUSSELL
    Reproduced by A. T. Clarke and Company.
    "Molly has never been false, she declares,
    Since the last time we parted at Wapping Old Stairs." Drawn by W. THOMAS SMITH
    Reproduced by Angerer and Göschl.
"Now like a mighty wind they raise to heaven the voice of song." Drawn by F. H. CRAWFORD
    Reproduced by the Swan Electric Engraving Company.

A LONDON GARLAND

	PAGE
inster Bridge. Drawn by EDGAR WILSON	91
Reproduced by Angerer and Göschl.	
ermaid Tavern. Drawn by R. BURNS	92
Reproduced by André and Sleigh.	
Fight." Drawn by FRANK DAD, R.I.	94
Reproduced by Angerer and Göschl.	
"To watch him strip his well-trained form, White, glowing, muscular, and warm." Drawn by JACK B. YEATS	96
Reproduced by Angerer and Göschl.	
k-out. Drawn by A. S. HARTRICK	97
Reproduced by Angerer and Göschl.	
y at the Nore. Drawn by R. VICAT COLE	99
Reproduced by Angerer and Göschl.	
a doleful tragedy." Drawn by W. RAINEY, R.I.	102
Reproduced by Walker and Boutall.	
lad of Guy Fawkes." Drawn by A. RACKHAM	104
Reproduced by Waterlow and Sons, Limited.	
ennel's macaw." Drawn by RONALD GRAY	106
Reproduced by Waterlow and Sons, Limited.	
"The splendour That beamed in the Spanish Bazaar; Where I purchased—my heart was so tender— A card-case, a pasteboard guitar, A bottle of perfume, a girdle." Drawn by H. TONKS	109
Reproduced by A. T. Clarke and Company.	
"O that 'twere possible . . . To find the arms of my true love." Drawn by EVERARD HOPKINS	112
Reproduced by Angerer and Göschl.	
"It leads me forth at evening, . . . When all my spirit reels At the shouts, the leagues of lights, And the roaring of the wheels." Drawn by FRED. T. JANE	115
Reproduced by Angerer and Göschl.	
ing on a tree root." Drawn by A. S. BOYD	119
Reproduced by Angerer and Göschl.	
ut Saint Martin's merry chimes." Drawn by ARCHIE MACGREGOR	126
Reproduced by the Swan Electric Engraving Company.	
thus this shadow . . . has been shed the same . . . from lamps which came for prayer." awn by HAL HURST	129
Reproduced by Angerer and Göschl.	
mes's Street." "For Fashion still is seen there." Drawn by J. W. T. MANUEL	137
Reproduced by A. and C. Dawson.	

LIST OF ILLUSTRATIONS

"She stands in despair
On the kerb." Drawn by A. H. COLLINGS
Reproduced by André and Sleigh.

"Quick, stranger, advance
To her aid." Drawn by OSCAR ECKHARDT
Reproduced by the Swan Electric Engraving Company.

Waiting for a Bus. Drawn by Sir J. D. LINTON
Reproduced by Walker and Boutall.

"Sunday at Hampstead." Drawn by L. RAVEN HILL .
Reproduced by A. T. Clarke and Company.

Tailpiece. Drawn by PHIL MAY . .
Reproduced by Angerer and Göschl.

"A London Plane-Tree." Drawn by J. BARNARD DAVIS
Reproduced by Angerer and Göschl.

"A Dream." Drawn by W. BAYES . . .
Reproduced by the Swan Electric Engraving Company.

"Queen at a pic-nic, leader of the glees." Drawn by G. D. HAMMOND
Reproduced by the Swan Electric Engraving Company.

"An Autumn Idyll." Drawn by FRED PEGRAM
Reproduced by Angerer and Göschl.

"I wot that I shall die of Love." Drawn by G. H. EDWARDS .
Reproduced by the Swan Electric Engraving Company.

"We aren't no thin red 'erocs." Drawn by W. B. WOLLEN, R.I.
Reproduced by Angerer and Göschl.

"Then it's Tommy this, an' Tommy that, an' 'Tommy, 'ow's yer soul?'" Drawn by T. S. C. CROWTHER . . . .
Reproduced by Angerer and Göschl.

"A Day at Hampton Court." Drawn by W. HATHERELL, R.I.
Reproduced by Angerer and Göschl.

Church of All Hallowes, Bread Street (now pulled down). Drawn by C. E. MALLOWS
Reproduced by Waterlow and Sons, Limited.

St. Helen's Church, Bishopsgate (interior). Drawn by R. STRUDWICK .
Reproduced by the Swan Electric Engraving Company.

"In the Rain." Drawn by CHADWELL SMITH .
Reproduced by Angerer and Göschl.

"Two stately swans! . . . Whence came they?" Drawn by A. HUGH FISHER
Reproduced by Angerer and Göschl.

"Fountain Court." Drawn by W. E. HOME .
Reproduced by Angerer and Göschl.

"A Loafer." Drawn by J. F. SULLIVAN . .
Reproduced by A. T. Clarke and Company.

A LONDON GARLAND

	PAGE
ing about the streets all day." Drawn by W. LUKER	183
Reproduced by André and Sleigh.	
from a house in Buckingham Street where once lived Charles Locke, and introduced into *David Copperfield*. Drawn by W. L. WYLLIE, A.R.A.	184
Reproduced by Angerer and Göschl.	
from a house in Buckingham Street where once lived Charles Locke, and introduced into *David Copperfield* (evening). Drawn by W. L. WYLLIE . . .	185
Reproduced by Angerer and Göschl.	
en fans for a penny are sold in the Strand!" Drawn by ENOCH WARD	186
Reproduced by Angerer and Göschl.	
"Where from some corner I can stare Across that line of yellow fire." Drawn by PAUL RENOUARD	188
Reproduced by Angerer and Göschl.	
"And I can see you, when I please, Behind the level lamps at night." Drawn by W. D. ALMOND	190
Reproduced by Waterlow and Sons, Limited.	
t Distance." Drawn by AUBREY BEARDSLEY	191
Reproduced by Angerer and Göschl.	
: Little Dancers." Drawn by A. S. HARTRICK	193
Reproduced by Angerer and Göschl.	
"The River, jaded and forlorn, Welters and wanders wearily." Drawn by J. M'NEIL WHISTLER	194
Reproduced by the Swan Electric Engraving Company.	
turn." Drawn by ARTHUR TOMSON . . .	196
Reproduced by the Swan Electric Engraving Company.	
tminster." Drawn by JOSEPH PENNELL . . .	198
Reproduced by the Swan Electric Engraving Company.	
." Drawn by JOSEPH PENNELL	200
Reproduced by the Swan Electric Engraving Company.	
: End." Drawn by R. A. BELL	203
Reproduced by Waterlow and Sons, Limited.	

E. A. Abbey, R.W.S.
Cecil Aldin
W. D. Almond
W. Bayes
Aubrey Beardsley
R. A. Bell
A. S. Boyd
R. Burns
R. Vicat Cole
A. H. Collings
Walter Crane, A.R.W.S.
F. H. Crawford
J. S. Crompton
T. S. C. Crowther
Frank Dad, R.I.
J. Barnard Davis
Oscar Eckhardt
G. H. Edwards
Frank L. Emanuel
A. J. Finberg
J. Finnemore
A. Hugh Fisher
J. Fulleylove, R.I.
Ronald Gray
Sir Francis Seymour Haden, P.R.P.E.
G. C. Haité
Chris Hammond

G. D. Hammond
A. S. Hartrick
W. Hatherell, R.I.
E. G. Hill
L. Raven Hill
W. E. Home
Everard Hopkins
Hal Hurst
Fred T. Jane
H. Johnson
F. W. Lawson
Sir J. D. Linton, P.R.I.
W. Luker
Robert W. Macbeth, A.R.A., F
Archie Macgregor
D. Macpherson
C. E. Mallows
G. Grenville Manton
J. W. T. Manuel
Phil May
H. R. Millar
E. H. New
Alfred Parsons, R.I.
J. Bernard Partridge
A. Pearse
Fred Pegram
Joseph Pennell

A LONDON GARLAND

R. Quinton
R. Rackham
Rainey, R.I.
̶eid
̶l Renouard
W. Russell
̶derick Sandys
̶ude A. Shepperson
̶dwell Smith
Thomas Smith
S. Stacey
Strudwick
J. Sullivan

J. F. Sullivan
Arthur Tomson
H. Tonks
F. H. Townsend
Enoch Ward
J. R. Way
J. M'Neil Whistler
W. Gleeson White
Edgar Wilson
W. B. Wollen, R.I.
Alice B. Woodward
W. L. Wyllie, A.R.A.
Jack B. Yeats

LIST OF AUTHORS

̶tthew Arnold
̶lliam Pulteney, Earl of Bath
̶ncis Beaumont
̶L. Binyon
̶lliam Blake
̶lfrid Scawen Blunt
̶ert Bridges
̶xander Brome
̶rge Gordon Byron, Lord Byron
̶ry Carey
̶offrey Chaucer
William Davenant
̶n Davidson
̶arles Dibdin
̶stin Dobson
̶hael Drayton
̶lliam Dunbar
̶ry Fielding
̶n Fletcher
̶n Gay
̶ver Goldsmith
̶omas Gray
̶eph Hall
E. Henley
̶bert Herrick
̶omas Hood
̶omas Hudson
̶n Jonson
̶n Keats

Rudyard Kipling
Andrew Lang
Henry S. Leigh
Amy Levy
Frederick Locker-Lampson
Justin Huntly M'Carthy
Rosamond Marriott-Watson
John Milton
Captain Charles Morris
William Morris
Thomas Nashe
Alexander Pope
Winthrop Mackworth Praed
John Hamilton Reynolds
John Wilmot, Earl of Rochester
Dante Gabriel Rossetti
William Shenstone
Edmund Spenser
J. Ashby-Sterry
Sir John Suckling
Henry Howard, Earl of Surrey
Jonathan Swift
Arthur Symons
Alfred Tennyson
James Thomson
Thomas Tickell
William Watson
William Wordsworth

A LONDON PRENTICE

PRENTIS whylom dwelled in our citee,
And of a craft of vitaillers was he;
Gaillard he was as goldfinch in the shawe,
Broun as a berie, a propre short felawe,
With lokkës blake, y-kempt ful fetisly.
Dauncen he coude so wel and iolily,
That he was clepéd Perkin Revelour.
He was as ful of love and paramour
As is the hyvë ful of hony swete;
Wel was the wenchë with him mightë mete.
At every brydale wolde he singe and hoppe,
He lovéd bet the taverne than the shoppe.

For whan ther any ryding was in Chepe,
Out of the shoppë thider wolde he lepe.
Til that he haddë al the sighte y-seyn,
And dauncéd wel, he wolde nat come ageyn.
And gadered him a meinee of his sort
To hoppe and singe, and maken swich disport.
And ther they setten steven for to mete
To pleyen at the dys in swich a strete.
For in the tounë nas ther no prentys,
That fairer coudë caste a paire of dys
Than Perkin coude, and ther-to he was free
Of his dispense, in place of privetee.
That fond his maister wel in his chaffare;
For often tyme he fond his box ful bare.
For sikerly a prentis revelour,
That haunteth dys, riot, or paramour,
His maister shal it in his shoppe abye,
Al have he no part of the minstralcye;
For thefte and riot, they ben convertible,
Al conne he pleye on giterne or ribible.

A LONDON GARLAND

Revel and trouthe, as in a low degree,
They ben ful wrothe al day, as men may see.
This ioly prentis with his maister bood,
Til he were ny out of his prentishood,
Al were he snibbéd bothe erly and late,
And somtyme lad with revel to Newgate;
But atté laste his maister him bithoghte,
Up-on a day, whan he his paper soghte,
Of a proverbë that seith this same word,
"Wel bet is roten appel out of hord
Than that it rotie al the remënaunt."
So fareth it by a riotous servaunt;
It is wel lassë harm to lete him pace,
Than he shende alle the servaunts in the place.
Therfore his maister yaf him acquitance,
And bad him go with sorwe and with meschance;
And thus this ioly prentis hadde his leve.
Now lat him riote al the night or leve.

GEOFFREY CHAUCER
(1340-1400).

IN PRAISE OF LONDON

ONDON, thou art of townës *A per se*.
   Soveraign of cities, semeliest in sight,
   Of high renoun, riches, and royaltie ;
   Of lordis, barons, and many goodly knyght ;
   Of most delectable lusty ladies bright ;
Of famous prelatis, in habitis clericall ;
   Of merchauntis full of substaunce and myght :
London, thou art the Flour of Cities all.

Gladdith anon thou lusty Troynovaunt,
   Citie that some tyme clepéd was New Troy,
In all the erth, imperiall as thou stant,
   Pryncesse of townes, of pleasure, and of joy,
   A richer restith under no Christen roy ;
For manly power, with craftis naturall,
   Fourmeth none fairer sith the flode of Noy :
London, thou art the Flour of Cities all.

Gemme of all joy, jasper of jocunditie,
   Most myghty carbuncle of vertue and valour ,
Strong Troy in vigour and in strenuytie ;
   Of royall cities rose and geraflour ;
   Empresse of townës, exalt in honour,
In beawtie berying the crone imperiall ;
   Swete paradise, precelling in pleasure :
London, thou art the Flour of Cities all.

Aboue all ryuers thy Ryuer hath renowne,
   Whose beryall stremys, pleasant and preclare,
Under thy lusty wallys renneth down,
   Where many a swanne doth swymme with wingïs fare ;

A LONDON GARLAND

Where many a barge doth saile, and row with are,
Where many a ship doth rest with toppe-royall.
 O ! towne of townes, patrone and but compare :
London, thou art the Flour of Cities all.

Upon thy lusty Brigge of pylers white
 Been merchauntïs full royall to behold ;
Upon thy stretis goeth many a semely knyght
 (All clad) in velvet gownes and cheynes of gold.
 By Julyus Cesar thy Tour founded of old
May be the Hous of Mars victoryall,
 Whos artillary with tonge may not be told :
London, thou art the Flour of Cities all.

Strong be thy wallys that about thee stand*i*s ;
 Wise be the people that within thee dwell*i*s ;
Fresh is thy ryver with his lusty strand*i*s ;
 Blith be thy churches, wele sownyng thy bell*i*s ;
 Riche be thy merchauntis in substaunce that excell*i*s ;
Fair be their wives, right lovesom, white and small ;
 Clere be thy virgyns, lusty under kell*i*s :
London, thou art the Flour of Cities all.

Thy famous Maire, by pryncely governaunce,
 With swerd of justice the ruleth prudently.
No Lord of Paris, Venyce, or Floraunce
 In dygnitie or honoure goeth to hym nye.
 He is exampler, loodë-ster, and guye,
Principall patrone and roose orygynalle,
 Above all Maires as maister moost worthy
London, thou art the Flour of Cities all.

WILLIAM DUNBAR
(1465-1530).

WINDSOR CASTLE

(Imprisoned in Windsor, the Lover recounteth his Pleasure there passed)

O cruel prison how could betide, alas !
As proud Windsor ?   Where I in lust and joy,
With a king's son, my childish years did pass,
In greater feast than Priam's sons of Troy ;
Where each sweet place returns a taste full sour.
The large green courts, where we were wont to rove,
With eyes upcast unto the maidens' tower,
And easy sighs, such as folk draw in love.
The stately seats, the ladies bright of hue,
The dances short, long tales of great delight ;
With words and looks that tigers could but rue,
When each of us did plead the other's right.
The palm play, where desported for the game,
With dazed eyes oft we, by gleams of love,
Have missed the ball, and got sight of our dame,
To bait her eyes, which kept the leads above.
The gravelled ground, with sleeves tied on the helm,
On foaming horse with swords and friendly hearts ;
With cheer as though one should another whelm,
Where we have fought, and chaséd oft with darts.
With silver drops the meads yet spread for ruth ;
In active games of nimbleness and strength,
Where we did strain, trainéd with swarms of youth,
Our tender limbs that yet shot up in length.
The secret groves, which oft we made resound
Of pleasant plaint, and of our ladies' praise ;
Recording oft what grace each one had found,
What hope of speed, what dread of long delays.
The wild forést, the clothéd holts with green ;
With reins availed, and swift ybreathéd horse,

With cry of hounds, and merry blasts between,
Where we did chase the fearful hart of force.
The void walls eke that harboured us each night :
Wherewith, alas ! revive within my breast
The sweet accord, such sleeps as yet delight ;
The pleasant dreams, the quiet bed of rest ;
The secret thoughts, imparted with such trust ;
The wanton talk, the divers change of play ;
The friendship sworn, each promise kept so just,
Wherewith we passed the winter night away.
And with this thought the blood forsakes the face ;
The tears berain my cheeks of deadly hue :
The which, as soon as sobbing sighs, alas !
Up-suppéd have, thus I my plaint renew :
" O place of bliss ! renewer of my woes !
Give me account, where is my noble fere ?
Whom in thy walls thou dost each night enclose ;
To other lief ; but unto me most dear."
Echo, alas ! that doth my sorrow rue,
Returns thereto a hollow sound of plaint.
Thus I alone, where all my freedom grew,
In prison pine, with bondage and restraint ;
And with remembrance of the greater grief,
To banish the less, I find my chief relief.

HENRY HOWARD, EARL OF SURRE
(1517-1546).

PROTHALAMION

Or, a Spousall Verse

of the double mariage of the two honorable and vertuous ladies, the Ladie Elizabeth, the Ladie Katherine Somerset, daughters to the Right Honourable the Earle of :ester, and espoused to the two worthie gentlemen M. Henry Gilford, and M. William ', Esquyers.

CALME was the day, and through the trembling ayre
Sweete-breathing Zephyrus did softly play
A gentle spirit, that lightly did delay
Hot Titan's beames, which then did glyster fayre ;
When I, (whom sullein care,
Through discontent of my long fruitlesse stay
In Prince's Court, and expectation vayne
Of idle hopes, which still doe fly away,
Like empty shaddowes, did afflict my brayne,)
Walkt forth to ease my payne
Along the shoare of silver streaming Themmes ;
Whose rutty Bancke, the which his River hemmes,
Was paynted all with variable flowers,
And all the meades adornd with daintie gemmes
Fit to decke maydens' bowres,
And crowne their Paramours
Against the Brydale day, which is not long :
   Sweete Themmes! runne softly, till I end my Song.

There, in a Meadow, by the River's side,
A Flocke of Nymphes I chauncéd to espy,
All lovely Daughters of the Flood thereby,
With goodly greenish locks, all loose untyde,
As each had bene a Bryde ;
And each one had a little wicker basket,
Made of fine twigs, entrayled curiously,

In which they gathered flowers to fill their flasket,
And with fine Fingers cropt full feateously
The tender stalkes on hye.
Of every sort, which in that Meadow grew,
They gathered some ; the Violet, pallid blew,
The little Dazie, that at evening closes,
The virgin Lillie, and the Primrose trew,
With store of vermeil Roses,
To decke their Bridegromes' posies
Against the Brydale day, which was not long :
   Sweete Themmes ! runne softly, till I end my Song.

With that I saw two Swannes of goodly hewe
Come softly swimming downe along the Lee ;
Two fairer Birds I yet did never see ;
The snow, which doth the top of Pindus strew,
Did never whiter shew,
Nor Jove himselfe, when he a Swan would be
For love of Leda, whiter did appeare ;
Yet Leda was (they say) as white as he,
Yet not so white as these, nor nothing neare ;
So purely white they were,
That even the gentle streame, the which them bare,
Seem'd foule to them, and bad his billowes spare
To wet their silken feathers, least they might
Soyle their fayre plumes with water not so fayre,
And marre their beauties bright,
That shone as heaven's light,
Against their Brydale day, which was not long :
   Sweete Themmes ! runne softly, till I end my Song.

Eftsoones the Nymphes, which now had Flowers their fill,
Ran all in haste to see that silver brood,
As they came floating on the Christal Flood ;
Whom when they sawe, they stood amazed still,
Their wondring eyes to fill ;
Them seem'd they never saw a sight so fayre,
Of Fowles, so lovely, that they sure did deeme
Them heavenly borne, or to be that same payre
Which through the Skie draw Venus' silver Teeme ;
For sure they did not seeme
To be begot of any earthly Seede,
But rather Angels, or of Angels' breede ;
Yet were they bred of Somer's heat, they say,

In sweetest Season, when each Flower and weede
The earth did fresh aray ;
So fresh they seem'd as day,
Even as their **Brydale day**, which was not long :
    Sweete Themmes ! runne softly, till I end my Song.

Then forth they all out of their baskets drew
Great store of Flowers, the honour of the field,
That to the sense did fragrant odours yeild,
All which upon those goodly Birds they threw
And all the Waves did strew,
That like old Peneus' Waters they did seeme,
When downe along by pleasant Tempe's shore,
Scattred with Flowres, through Thessaly they streeme,
That they appeare, through Lillies' plenteous store,
Like a Bryde's Chamber flore.
Two of those Nymphes, meane while, two Garlands bound
Of freshest Flowres which in that Mead they found,
The which presenting all in trim Array,
Their snowie Foreheads therewithall they crownd,
Whil'st one did sing this Lay,
Prepar'd against that Day,
Against their **Brydale day**, which was not long :
    Sweete Themmes ! runne softly till I end my Song.

" Ye gentle Birdes ! the world's faire ornament,
And heaven's glorie, whom this happie hower
Doth leade unto your lovers' blisfull bower,
Joy may you have, and gentle heart's content
Of your love's couplement ;
And let faire Venus, that is Queene of love,
With her heart-quelling Sonne upon you smile,
Whose smile, they say, hath vertue to remove
All Love's dislike, and friendship's faultie guile
For ever to assoile.
Let endlesse Peace your steadfast hearts accord,
And blessed Plentie wait upon your bord ;
And let your bed with pleasures chast abound,
That fruitfull issue may to you afford,
Which may your foes confound,
And make your joyes redound
Upon your **Brydale day**, which is not long
    Sweete Themmes ! runne softlie, till I end my Song."

So ended she ; and all the rest around
To her redoubled that her undersong,
Which said their brydale daye should not be long :
And gentle Eccho from the neighbour ground
Their accents did resound.
So forth those joyous Birdes did passe along,
Adowne the Lee, that to them murmurde low,
As he would speake, but that he lackt a tong,
Yet did by signes his glad affection show,
Making his streame run slow.
And all the foule which in his flood did dwell
Gan flock about these twaine, that did excell
The rest, so far as Cynthia doth shend
The lesser starres. So they, enranged well,
Did on those two attend,
And their best service lend
Against their wedding day, which was not long :
   Sweete Themmes ! run softly, till I end my Song.

At length they all to mery London came,
To mery London, my most kyndly Nurse,
That to me gave this Life's first native sourse,
Though from another place I take my name,
An house of aunceint fame :
There when they came, whereas those bricky towres
The which on Themmes brode aged backe doe ryde,
Where now the studious Lawyers have their bowers,
There whylome wont the Templer Knights to byde,
Till they decayd through pride :
Next whereunto there standes a stately place,
Where oft I gayned giftes and goodly grace
Of that great Lord, which therein wont to dwell,
Whose want too well now feeles my freendles case ;
But ah ! here fits not well
Olde woes, but joyes, to tell
Against the bridale daye, which is not long :
   Sweete Themmes ! runne softly, till I end my Song.

Yet therein now doth lodge a noble Peer,
Great England's glory, and the World's wide wonder,
Whose dreadfull name late through all Spaine did thunder,
And Hercules' two pillors standing neere
Did make to quake and feare :
Faire branch of Honor, flower of Chevalrie !

A LONDON GARLAND

That fillest England with thy triumphe's fame,
Joy have thou of thy noble victorie,
And endlesse happinesse of thine owne name
That promiseth the same ;
That through thy prowesse, and victorious armes
Thy country may be freed from forraine harmes ;
And great Elisa's glorious name may ring
Through al the world, fil'd with thy wide Alarmes,
Which some brave muse may sing
To ages following.
Upon the Brydale day, which is not long :
   Sweete Themmes ! runne softly till I end my Song.

From those high Towers this noble Lord issuing,
Like Radiant Hesper, when his golden hayre
In th' Ocean billowes he hath bathéd fayre,
Descended to the River's open vewing,
With a great traine ensuing.
Above the rest were goodly to bee seene
Two gentle Knights of lovely face and feature,
Beseeming well the bower of anie Queene,
With gifts of wit, and ornaments of nature,
Fit for so goodly stature,
That like the twins of Jove they seem'd in sight,
Which decke the Bauldricke of the Heavens bright ;
They two, forth pacing to the River's side,
Received those two faire Brides, their Loves delight ;
Which, at th' appointed tyde,
Each one did make his Bryde
Against their Brydale day, which is not long :
   Sweete Themmes ! runne softly, till I end my Song.

                          EDMUND SPENS
                          (1552-1599).

WINDSOR FOREST

BY this, the wedding ends, and brake up all the show :
And Thames, got, born, and bred, immediately doth flow
To Windsor-ward amain (that with a wond'ring eye,
The forest might behold his awful empery),
And soon becometh great, with waters wext so rank,
That with his wealth he seems to retch his wid'ned bank ;
Till happily attain'd his grandsire Chiltern's grounds,
Who with his beechen wreaths this king of rivers crowns.
Amongst his holts and hills, as on his way he makes,
At Reading once arriv'd, clear Kennet overtakes
Her lord, the stately Thames, which that great flood again,
With many signs of joy, doth kindly entertain.
Then Loddon next comes in, contributing her store ;
As still we see, the much runs ever to the more.
    Set out with all this pomp, when this imperial stream
Himself establish'd sees amidst his wat'ry realm,

His much-lov'd Henley leaves, and proudly doth pursue
His wood-nymph Windsor's seat, her lovely site to view.
Whose most delightful face when once the river sees,
Which shows herself attir'd in tall and stately trees,
He in such earnest love with amorous gestures wooes,
That looking still at her, his way was like to lose ;
And wand'ring in and out, so wildly seems to go,
As headlong he himself into her lap would throw.
    Him with the like desire the forest doth embrace,
And with her presence strives her Thames as much to grace.
No forest, of them all, so fit as she doth stand,
When princes, for their sports, her pleasures will command ;
No wood-nymph as herself such troops hath ever seen,
Nor can such quarries boast as have in Windsor been ;
Not any ever had so many solemn days,
So brave assemblies view'd, nor took so rich assays.
    Then hand in hand, her Thames the forest softly brings
To that supremest place of the great English kings,
The Garter's royal seat, from him who did advance
That princely order first, our first that conquer'd France ;
The temple of Saint George, whereas his honour'd knights,
Upon his hallow'd day, observe their ancient rites ;
Where Eaton is at hand to nurse that learned brood,
To keep the Muses still near to this princely flood ;
That nothing there may want, to beautify that seat,
With every pleasure stor'd : and here my song complete.

                              MICHAEL DRAYT<
                              (1563-1631).

WINDSOR TO LONDON THAMES

BUT now this mighty flood, upon his voyage prest
(That found how with his strength, his beauties still increa
From where brave Windsor stood on tip-toe to behold
The fair and goodly Thames, so far as ere he could,
     With kingly houses crown'd, of more than earthly pride,
Upon his either banks, as he along doth glide),
With wonderful delight doth his long course pursue,
Where Oatlands, Hampton Court, and Richmond he doth view,
Then Westminster the next great Thames doth entertain ;
That vaunts her palace large, and her most sumptuous fane :
The land's tribunal seat that challengeth for her's,

The crowning of our kings, their famous sepulchres.
Then goes he on along by that more beauteous strand,
Expressing both the wealth and bravery of the land.
(So many sumptuous bowers, within so little space,
The all-beholding Sun scarce sees in all his race.)
And on by London leads, which like a crescent lies,
Whose windows seem to mock the star-befreckled skies ;
Besides her rising spires, so thick themselves that show,
As do the bristling reeds within his banks that grow.
There sees his crowded wharfs, and people-pest'red shores,
His bosom over-spread with shoals of labouring oars :
With that most costly bridge that doth him most renown,
By which he clearly puts all other rivers down.

MICHAEL DRAYTON.

A WINTER SONG

AUTUMN hath all the summer's fruitful treasure;
Gone is our sport, fled is our Croydon's pleasure!
Short days, sharp days, long nights come on apace
Ah, who shall hide us from the winter's face?
Cold doth increase, the sickness will not cease,
And here we lie, God knows, with little ease.
From winter, plague, and pestilence, good Lord, deliver us!

London doth mourn, Lambeth is quite forlorn!
Trades cry, woe worth that ever they were born!
The want of term is town and city's harm;
Close chambers we do want to keep us warm.
Long banishéd must we live from our friends:
This low-built house will bring us to our ends.
From winter, plague, and pestilence, good Lord, deliver us!

THOMAS NASH
(1567-1600).

SONG: TO CELIA

ISS me, sweet : the wary lover
Can your favours keepe, and cover,
When the common courting jay
All your bounties will betray.
Kiss againe : no creature comes.
Kisse, and score up wealthy summes
On my lips, thus hardly sundred,
While you breathe.   First give a hundred,
Then a thousand, then another
Hundred, then unto the tother
Adde a thousand, and so more :
Till you equall with the store,
All the grasse that Rumney yeelds,
Or the sands in Chelsey Fields,
Or the drops in silver Thames,
Or the stars, that gild his streames,
In the silent summer-nights,
When youths ply their stolen delights.
That the curious may not know
How to tell 'hem as they flow,
And the envious, when they find
What their number is, be pin'd.

BEN JONSON
(1573-1637).

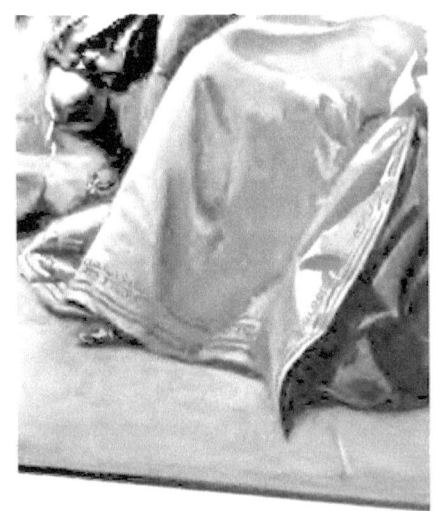

21

IN LONDON WAY

FIE on all courtesie, and unruly windes,
Two onely foes that faire disguisement findes !
Strange curse ! but fit for such a fickle age,
When scalpes are subject to such vassalage.
Late travaling along in London way,
Mee met, as seem'd by his disguis'd array,
A lustie courtier, whose curléd head
With abron locks was fairely furnishéd.
I him saluted in our lavish wise :
He answeres my untimely courtesies.
His bonnet vail'd, ere ever he could thinke,
Th' unruly winde blowes off his periwinke.
He lights and runs, and quickly hath him sped,
To overtake his over-running head.
The sportfull winde, to mocke the headlesse man,
Tosses apace his pitch'd Rogerian :
And straight it to a deeper ditch hath blowne ;
There must my yonker fetch his waxen crowne.
I lookt and laught, whiles in his raging minde,
He curst all courtesie, and unruly winde.
I lookt and laught, and much I mervailéd,
To see so large a caus-way in his head.
And me bethought, that when it first begon,
'Twas some shrewd autumne that so bar'd the bone.
Is't not sweete pride, when men their crownes must shade,
With that which jerks the hams of every jade,
Or floor-strow'd locks from off the barber's sheares ?
But waxen crownes well gree with borrow'd haires.

Joseph Hall
(1574-1656).

THE MAY-LORD

ONDON, to thee I do present
The merry month of May;
Let each true subject be content
To hear me what I say:
For from the top of conduit-head,
As plainly may appear,
I will both tell my name to you,
And wherefore I came here.
My name is Ralph, by due descent
Though not ignoble I,
Yet far inferior to the flock
Of gracious grocery;
And by the common counsel of
My fellows in the Strand,
With gilded staff and crossed scarf,
The May-lord here I stand.
Rejoice, O English hearts, rejoice!
Rejoice, O lovers dear!
Rejoice, O city, town, and country!
Rejoice eke every shire!
For now the fragrant flowers do spring
And sprout in seemly sort,
The little birds do sit and sing,
The lambs do make fine sport;
And now the birchen-tree doth bud,
And makes the schoolboy cry;
The morris rings, while hobby-horse
Doth foot it feateously;
The lords and ladies now abroad,
For their disport and play,
Do kiss sometimes upon the grass,

And sometimes in the hay.
Now butter with a leaf of sage
Is good to purge the blood;
Fly Venus and phlebotomy,
For they are neither good!
Now little fish on tender stone
Begin to cast their bellies,
And sluggish snails, that erst were mewed,
Do creep out of their shellies;
The rumbling rivers now do warm,
For little boys to paddle;
The sturdy steed now goes to grass,
And up they hang his saddle;
The heavy hart, the bellowing buck,
The rascal, and the pricket,
Are now among the yeoman's pease,
And leave the fearful thicket;
And be like them, O you, I say,
Of this same noble town,
And lift aloft your velvet heads,
And slipping off your gown,
With bells on legs, and napkins clean
Unto your shoulders tied,
With scarfs and garters as you please,
And "Hey for our town!" cried,
March out, and show your willing minds,
By twenty and by twenty,
To Hogsdon, or to Newington,
Where ale and cakes are plenty;
And let it ne'er be said for shame,
That we, the youths of London,
Lay thrumming of our caps at home,
And left our custom undone.
Up then, I say, both young and old,
Both man and maid a-maying,
With drums and guns that bounce aloud,
And merry tabor playing!
Which to prolong, God save our King,
And send his country peace,
And root out treason from the land!
And so, my friends, I cease.

JOHN FLETCHER
(1576-1625).

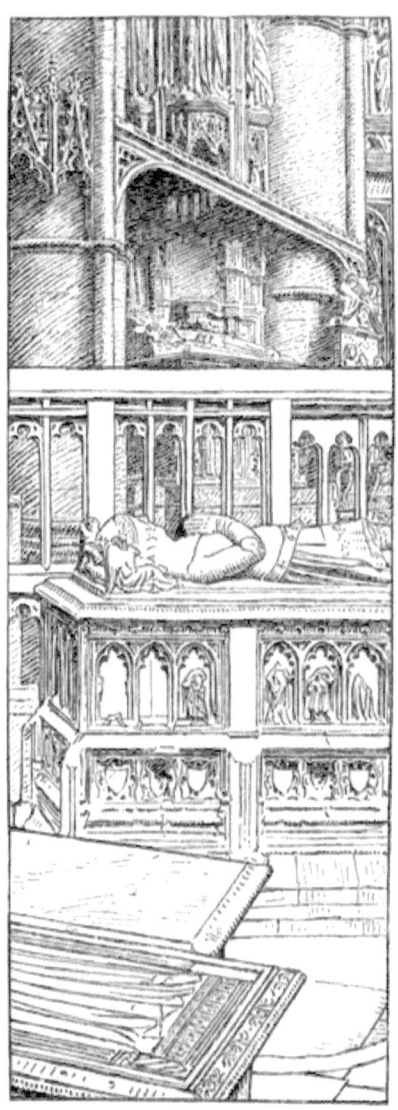

LINES ON THE TOMBS IN WESTMINSTER

MORTALITY, behold and fear !
What a change of flesh is here !
Think how many royal bones
Sleep within this heap of stones ;
Here they lie had realms and lands,
Who now want strength to stir their hands ;
Where from their pulpits seal'd with dust
They preach, "In greatness is no trust."
Here's an acre sown indeed
With the richest, royall'st seed
That the earth did e'er suck in,
Since the first man died for sin :
Here the bones of birth have cried,
"Though gods they were, as men they died : "
Here are sands, ignoble things,
Dropt from the ruin'd sides of kings :
Here's a world of pomp and state,
Buried in dust, once dead by fate.

FRANCIS BEAUMONT
(1586-1616).

TEARES TO THAMASIS

SEND, I send here my supremest kiss
To thee, my silver-footed Thamasis.
No more shall I reiterate thy strand,
Whereon so many stately structures stand :
Nor in the summer's sweeter evenings go
To bath in thee, as thousand others doe :
No more shall I along thy christall glide,
In barge with boughes and rushes beautifi'd,
With soft-smooth virgins for our chast disport,
To Richmond, Kingstone, and to Hampton-Court :
Never againe shall I with finnie ore
Put from or draw unto the faithfull shore,
And landing here, or safely landing there,
Make way to my belovéd Westminster,
Or to the golden Cheap-side, where the earth
Of Julia Herrick gave to me my birth.
May all clean nimphs and curious water-dames
With swan-like state flote up and down thy streams :
No drought upon thy wanton waters fall
To make them leane and languishing at all :
No ruffling winds come hither to disease
Thy pure and silver-wristed Naides !
Keep up your state, ye streams ; and as ye spring,
Never make sick your banks by surfeiting !
Grow young with tydes, and though I see ye never,
Receive this vow, so fare ye well for ever !

ROBERT HERRICK
(1591-1674).

THE LONG VACATION IN LONDON

(In Verse Burlesque, or Mock Verse)

OW town-wit sayes to witty friend :
"Transcribe apace all thou hast pen'd ;
For I in journey hold it fit,
To cry thee up to countrey-wit.
Our mules are come ! dissolve the club !
The word, till term, is, 'Rub, O rub !' "—
Now gamester poor, in cloak of stammel,
Mounted on steed as slow as cammel,
Battoone of crab in luckless hand
(Which serves for bilboe and for wand),
Early in morne does sneak from town,
Least landlord's wife should seise on crown ;
On crown, which he in pouch does keep,
When day is done, to pay for sleep ;
For he in journey nought does eat.
Host spies him come, cryes : "Sir, what meat ?"
He calls for room, and down he lies.
Quoth host : "No supper, sir ?" He cryes :
"I eate no supper, fling on rug !
I'm sick, d'you hear ? yet bring a jug !"
Now damsel young, that dwels in Cheap,
For very joy begins to leap :
Her elbow small she oft does rub,
Tickled with hope of sillabub ;
For mother (who does gold maintain
On thumbe, and keys in silver chaine)
In snow white clout, wraps nook of pye,
Fat capon's wing, and rabbet's thigh,
And says to hackney coachman : "Go,
Take shillings six, say I, or no."

"Whither?" says he. Quoth she: "Thy teame
Shall drive to place where groweth creame."
But husband gray now comes to stall,
For prentice notch'd he straight does call:
"Where's dame?" quoth he. Quoth son of shop:
"She's gone her cake in milk to sop."
"Ho, ho! to Islington! enough!
Fetch Job, my son, and our dog Roffe!
For there in pond, through mire and muck,
We'l cry, 'Hay, duck! there, Ruffe! hay, duck!'"
Now Turnbull-dame, by starving paunch,
Bates two stone weight in either haunch:
On branne and liver she must dine,
And sits at dore instead of signe.
She softly says to roaring Swash,
Who wears long whiskers: "Go, fetch cash!
There's gown," quoth she, "speak broaker fair,
Till term brings up weak countrey heir:
Whom kirtle red will much amaze,
Whilst clown his man on signes does gaze,
In liv'ry short, galloone on cape,
With cloak-bag mounting high as nape."
Now man that trusts, with weary thighs,
Seeks garret where small poet lies:
He comes to Lane, finds garret shut;
Then, not with knuckle, but with foot,
He rudely thrusts, would enter dores;
Though poet sleeps not, yet he snores:
Cit chafes like beast of Libia; then
Sweares, he'l not come or send agen.
From little lump triangular
Poor poets' sighs are heard afar.
Quoth he: "Do noble numbers choose
To walk on feet, that have no shoose?"
Then he does wish with fervent breath,
And as his last request ere death,
Each ode a bond, each madrigal,
A lease from Haberdashers' Hall,
Or that he had protected bin
At Court, in list of Chamberlain;
For wights near thrones care not an ace
For Woodstreet friend, that wieldeth mace.
Courts pay no scores but when they list,
And treasurer still has cramp in fist:

Then forth he steales ; to Globe does run ;
And smiles, and vowes four acts are done ;
Finis to bring he does protest,
Tells ev'ry play'r his part is best ;
And all to get (as poets use)
Some coyne in pouche to solace Muse.
Now wight that acts on stage of Bull,
In skullers' bark does lie at hull,
Which he for pennies two does rig,
All day on Thames to bob for grig ;
Whilst fencer poor does by him stand,
In old dung-lighter, hook in hand,
Between knees rod, with canvas crib
To girdle tide, close under rib,
Where worms are put, which must small fish
Betray at night to earthen dish.
Now London's chief, on saddle new,
Rides into fair of Barthol'mew :
He twirles his chain, and looketh big,
As if to fright the head of pig,
That gaping lies on greasy stall
Till female with great belly call.
Now alderman in field does stand,
With foot on trig, a quoit in hand :
" I'm seven," quoth he, " the game is up !
Nothing I pay, and yet I sup."
To alderman quoth neighbour then :
" I lost but mutton, play for hen."
But wealthy blade cryes out : " At rate
Of kings, should'st play ? let's go, 'tis late ! "
Now lean atturney, that his cheese
Ne'er par'd, nor verses took for fees,
And aged proctor, that controules
The feats of punk in court of Paul's,
Do each with solemn oath agree
To meet in fields of Finsbury :
With loynes in canvas bow-case tyde,
Where arrows stick with mickle pride,
With hats pinn'd up, and bow in hand,
All day most fiercely there they stand,
Like ghosts of Adam Bell and Clymme :
Sol sets for fear they'l shoot at him.
Now spynie Ralph, and Gregorie small,
And short hayr'd Stephen, whay-fac'd Paul

(Whose times are out, indentures torn),
Who seven long years did never scorn
To fetch up coales for maids to use,
Wipe mistresses' and children's shooes,
Do jump for joy they are made free ;
Hire meagre steeds, to ride and see
Their parents old who dwell as near
As place call'd Peake in Derby-shire.
There they alight, old crones are milde,
Each weeps on cragg of pretty childe :
They portions give trades up to set,
That babes may live, serve God, and cheat.
Near house of law by Temple-Bar,
Now man of mace cares not how far,
In stockings blew he marcheth on,
With velvet cape his cloak upon :
In girdle, scrolls, where names of some
Are written down, whom touch of thumbe,
On shoulder left must safe convoy,
Anoying wights with name of Roy ;
Poor pris'ner's friend that sees the touch,
Cries out, aloud : "I thought as much !"
Now vaulter good, and dancing lass
On rope, and man that cryes " Hey, pass,"
And tumbler young that needs must stoop,
Lay head to heel to creep through hoope,
And man in chimney hid to dress,
Puppit that acts our old queen Bess,
And man that whilst the puppits play
Through nose expoundeth what they say,
And man that does in chest include
Old Sodom and Gomorrah lewd,
And white oate-eater that does dwell
In stable small, at sign of Bell,
That lift up hoope to show the prancks,
Taught by magitian stiled Banks
And ape, led captive still in chain
Till he renounce the pope and Spaine :
All these on hoof now trudge from town
To cheat poor turnip-eating clown.
Now man of war with visage red,
Growes cholerick and sweares for bread.
He sendeth note to man of kin,
But man leaves word : " I'm not within."

He meets in street with friend call'd Will,
And cryes : "Old rogue ! what, living still ?"
But ere that street they quite are past,
He softly asks : "What money hast ?"
Quoth friend : "A crown !"   He cryes : "Dear heart !
O base ! no more ! sweet, lend me part !"
But stay, my frightened pen is fled ;
Myself through fear creep under bed,
For just as Muse would scribble more,
Fierce city dunne did rap at door.

Sir William Davenant
(1605-1668).

A BALLAD UPON A WEDDING

TELL thee, Dick, where I have been,
Where I the rarest things have seen ;
O, things without compare !
Such sights again cannot be found
In any place on English ground,
Be it at wake or fair.

At Charing Cross, hard by the way
Where we (thou know'st) do sell our hay,
There is a house with stairs ;
And there did I see coming down
Such folks as are not in our town,
Vorty at least, in pairs.

Amongst the rest, one pest'lent fine
(His beard no bigger though than mine)
Walk'd on before the rest :
Our landlord looks like nothing to him :
The king (God bless him !) 'twould undo him :
Should he go still so drest.

At Course-a-park, without all doubt,
He should have first been taken out
By all the maids i' th' town :
Though lusty Roger there had been,
Or little George upon the green,
Or Vincent of the crown.

But wot you what ? the youth was going
To make an end of all his wooing ;
The parson for him staid :

Yet by his leave (for all his haste)
He did not so much wish all past
(Perchance) as did the maid.

The maid (and thereby hangs a tale)
For such a maid no Whitson-ale
Could ever yet produce :
No grape that's kindly ripe, could be
So round, so plump, so soft as she,
Nor half so full of juyce.

Her finger was so small, the ring
Would not stay on which they did bring
It was too wide a peck :
And to say truth (for out it must)
It look'd like the great collar (just)
About our young colt's neck.

Her feet beneath her petticoat,
Like little mice, stole in and out,
As if they fear'd the light :
But O! she dances such a way!
No sun upon an Easter Day
Is half so fine a sight.

Her cheeks so rare a white was on,
No daisie makes comparison ;
(Who sees them is undone)
For streaks of red were mingled there
Such as are on a Cath'rine pear,
(The side that's next the sun.)

Her lips were red ; and one was thin,
Compar'd to that was next her chin
(Some bee had stung it newly).
But (Dick) her eyes so guard her face,
I durst no more upon them gaze,
Than on the sun in July.

Her mouth so small, when she does speak,
Thou'd'st swear her teeth her words did break,
That they might passage get ;
But she so handled still the matter,
They came as good as ours, or better,
And are not spent a whit.

A LONDON GARLAND

If wishing should be any sin,
The parson himself had guilty been ;
(She look'd that day so purely :)
And did the youth so oft the feat
At night, as some did in conceit,
It would have spoil'd him, surely.

Passion, O me ! how I run on !
There's that that would be thought upon,
I trow besides the bride.
The business of the kitchen's great,
For it is fit that men should eat,
Nor was it there denied.

Just in the nick the cook knock'd thrice,
And all the waiters in a trice
His summons did obey ;
Each servingman with dish in hand,
March'd boldly up, like our train'd-band,
Presented, and away.

When all the meat was on the table,
What man of knife, or teeth, was able
To stay to be intreated ?
And this the very reason was,
Before the parson could say grace,
The company was seated.

Now hats fly off, and youths carouse ;
Healths first go round, and then the house,
The bride's came thick and thick ;
And when 'twas nam'd another's health,
Perhaps he made it hers by stealth
(And who could help it, Dick ?).

O' th' suddein up they rise and dance ;
Then sit again, and sigh, and glance ;
Then dance again, and kiss :
Thus sev'ral ways the time did pass,
Till ev'ry woman wish'd her place,
And ev'ry man wish'd his.

By this time all were stol'n aside
To counsel and undress the bride ;

But that he must not know :
But yet 'twas thought he guessed her mind,
And did not mean to stay behind
Above an hour or so.

When in he came (Dick) there she lay
Like new fal'n snow melting away
('Twas time, I trow to part) :
Kisses were now the only stay,
Which soon she gave, as who would say :
" Good boy ! with all my heart ! "

But just as Heav'ns would have to cross it,
In came the bride-maids with the posset :
The bridegroom eat in spight ;
For had he left the women to't
It would have cost two hours to do't,
Which were too much that night.

SIR JOHN SUCKLING
(1609-1641).

WHEN THE ASSAULT WAS INTENDED TO THE CITY

CAPTAIN or Colonel, or Knight in Arms,
    Whose chance on these defenceless doors may seize,
    If deed of honour did thee ever please,
    Guard them, and him within protect from harms.
He can requite thee ; for he knows the charms
That call fame on such gentle acts as these,
And he can spread thy name o'er lands and seas,
Whatever clime the sun's bright circle warms.
Lift not thy spear against the Muses' bower :
The great Emathian conqueror bid spare
The house of Pindarus, when temple and tower
Went to the ground ; and the repeated air
Of sad Electra's poet had the power
To save the Athenian walls from ruin bare.—JOHN MILTON
                                    (1608-1674).

A LONDON CAVALIER

(Written in 1645)

COME your ways,
   Bonny boys
   Of the town,
For now is your time or never.
   Shall your fears
   Or your cares
   Cast you down?
Hang your wealth
And your health.
Get renown,
We are all undone for ever.
Now the king and the crown
Are tumbling down,
And the realm doth groan with disasters,
And the scum of the land
Are the men that command,
And our slaves are become our masters.

Now our lives,
Children, wives
And estate,
Are a prey to the lust and plunder,
   To the rage
   Of our age :
   And the fate
   Of our land
   Is at hand :

'Tis too late
To tread these usurpers under.
First down goes the crown,
Then follows the gown,
Thus levell'd are we by the roundhead,
While church and state must
Feed their pride and their lust,
And the kingdom and king confounded.

Shall we still
Suffer ill
And be dumb?
And let every varlet undo us?
Shall we doubt
Of each lout,
That doth come,
With a voice
Like the noise
Of a drum,
And a sword or a buff coat to us?
Shall we lose our estates
By plunder and rates
To bedeck those proud upstarts that swagger?
Rather fight for your meat,
Which those locusts do eat,
Now every man's a beggar.

ALEXANDER BROME
(1620-1666).

A TOWN GALLANT

OOM for a brisk Blade of the Town
    That takes Delight in roaring,
Who all day rambles up and down,
    And at night in the street lies snoring !
That for the noble name of Spark
    Dares his Companions rally :
Commits an Outrage in the Dark,
    Then slinks into an Alley !

To every Female that he meets
    He swears he bears affection ;
Defies all Laws, Arrests, and Cheats
    By the Help of a kind Protection :
Till he, intending further Wrongs,
    By some resenting Cully
Is decently run through the lungs,
    And there is an End of Bully !

JOHN WILMOT, EARL OF ROC
(1647-1680).

A CITY SHOWER

CAREFUL observers may foretell the hour
(By sure prognostics) when to dread a shower.
While rain depends, the pensive cat gives o'er
Her frolics, and pursues her tail no more.
Returning home at night, you'll find the sink
Strike your offended sense with double stink.
If you be wise, then go not far to dine ;
You'll spend in coach-hire more than save in wine.
A coming shower your shooting corns presage,
Old aches will throb, your hollow tooth will rage.
Sauntering in coffee-house is Dulman seen ;
He damns the climate, and complains of spleen.
Meanwhile the south, rising with dabbled wings,
A sable cloud athwart the welkin flings,
That swill'd more liquor than it could contain,
And, like a drunkard, gives it up again.
Brisk Susan whips her linen from the rope,
While the first drizzling shower is borne aslope.
Such is that sprinkling which some careless quean
Flirts on you from her mop, but not so clean :
You fly, invoke the gods ; then, turning, stop

To rail; she, singing still, whirls on her mop.
Not yet the dust that shunn'd th' unequal strife,
But, aided by the wind, fought still for life;
And, wafted with its foe by violent gust,
'Twas doubtful which was rain, and which was dust.
Ah! where must needy poet seek for aid,
When dust and rain at once his coat invade?
Sole coat! where dust, cemented by the rain,
Erects the nap, and leaves a cloudy stain!
Now in contiguous drops the flood comes down,
Threatening with deluge this devoted town.
To shops in crowds the daggled females fly,
Pretend to cheapen goods, but nothing buy.
The Templar spruce, while every spout's abroach,
Stays till 'tis fair, yet seems to call a coach.
The tuck'd-up semstress walks with hasty strides,
While streams run down her oil'd umbrella's sides.
Here various kinds, by various fortunes led,
Commence acquaintance underneath a shed.
Triumphant Tories and desponding Whigs
Forget their feuds, and join to save their wigs.
Box'd in a chair, the beau impatient sits,
While spouts run clattering o'er the roof by fits,
And ever and anon with frightful din
The leather sounds; he trembles from within.
So when Troy chairmen bore the Wooden Steed,
Pregnant with Greeks impatient to be freed
(Those bully Greeks, who, as the moderns do,
Instead of paying chairmen, ran them through),
Laocoön struck the outside with his spear,
And each imprison'd hero quak'd for fear.

    Now from all parts the swelling kennels flow,
And bear their trophies with them as they go:
Filths of all hues and odours seem to tell
What street they sail'd from by their sight and smell.
They, as each torrent drives, with rapid force,
From Smithfield or St. 'Pulchres shape their course,
And in huge confluence join'd at Snowhill ridge,
Fall from the *conduit* prone to Holborn bridge.
Sweepings from butchers' stalls, dung, guts, and blood,
Drown'd puppies, stinking sprats, all drenched in mud,
Dead cats, and turnip-tops, come tumbling down the Flood.

JONATHAN SWIFT
(1667-1745).

A WOMAN OF FASHION

"THEN, behind, all my hair is done up in a plat,
And so, like a cornet's, tucked under my hat,
Then I mount on my palfrey as gay as a lark,
And, follow'd by John, take the dust in High Park.
In the way I am met by some smart macaroni,
Who rides by my side on a little bay pony—
No sturdy Hibernian, with shoulders so wide,
But as taper and slim as the ponies they ride ;
Their legs are as slim, and their shoulders no wider,
Dear sweet little creatures, both pony and rider !

" But sometimes, when hotter, I order my chaise,
And manage, myself, my two little greys ;
Sure never were seen two such sweet little ponies,
Other horses are clowns, and these macaronies,
And to give them this title, I'm sure isn't wrong,
Their legs are so slim, and their tails are so long.

" In Kensington Gardens to stroll up and down,
You know was the fashion before you left town,
The thing's well enough, when allowance is made
For the size of the trees and the depth of the shade.
But the spread of their leaves such a shelter affords
To those noisy impertinent creatures call'd birds,
Whose ridiculous chirruping ruins the scene,
Brings the country before me, and gives me the spleen.

" Yet, though 'tis too rural—to come near the mark,
We all herd in *one* walk, and that, nearest the Park,
There with ease we may see, as we pass by the wicket,
The chimneys of Knightsbridge, and—footmen at cricket.
I must though, in justice, declare that the grass,
Which, worn by our feet, is diminish'd apace,
In a little time more will be brown and as flat
As the sand at Vauxhall, or as Ranelagh mat.
Improving thus fast, perhaps, by degrees
We may see rolls and butter spread under the trees,
With a small pretty band in each seat of the walk,
To play little tunes and enliven our talk."

THOMAS TICKELL
(1686-1740).

HAMPTON COURT

CLOSE by those meads, for ever crown'd with flow'rs,
   Where Thames with pride surveys his rising tow'rs,
   There stands a structure of majestic frame,
   Which from the neighb'ring Hampton takes it's name.
   Here Britain's statesmen oft the fall foredoom
Of foreign tyrants and of nymphs at home;
Here thou, great ANNA! whom three realms obey,
Dost sometimes counsel take—and sometimes tea.
   Hither the heroes and the nymphs resort,
To taste awhile the pleasures of a Court;
In various talk th' instructive hours they past,
Who gave the ball, or paid the visit last;
One speaks the glory of the British Queen,
And one describes a charming Indian screen;
A third interprets motions, looks, and eyes;
At ev'ry word a reputation dies.
Snuff, or the fan, supply each pause of chat,
With singing, laughing, ogling, *and all that.*

                                ALEXANDER POPE
                                    (1688-1744).

NIGHTWALKING

WHEN Night first bids the twinkling stars appear,
    Or with her cloudy vest enwraps the air,
    Then swarms the busy street; with caution tread,
    Where the shop-windows[1] falling threat thy head;
    Now labourers home return and join their strength
To bear the tottering plank, or ladder's length;
Still fix thy eyes intent upon the throng,
And, as the passes open, wind along.
    Where the fair columns of St. Clement stand,
Whose straiten'd bounds encroach upon the Strand;
Where the low penthouse bows the walker's head,
And the rough pavement wounds the yielding tread;
Where not a post protects the narrow space,
And strung in twines, combs dangle in thy face;
Summon at once thy courage, rouze thy care,
Stand firm, look back, be resolute, beware.
Forth issuing from steep lanes, the collier's steeds
Drag the black load; another cart succeeds,
Team follows team, crowds heap'd on crowds appear,
And wait impatient till the road grow clear.
Now all the pavement sounds with trampling feet,
And the mix'd hurry barricades the street.
Entangled here, the waggon's lengthen'd team
Cracks the tough harness; here a ponderous beam
Lies over-turn'd athwart; for slaughter fed,
Here lowing bullocks raise their horned head.
Now oaths grow loud, with coaches coaches jar,
And the smart blow provokes the sturdy war;

[1] A species of window now almost forgotten.—N.

From the high box they whirl the thong around,
And with the twining lash their shins resound:
Their rage ferments, more dangerous wounds they try,
And the blood gushes down their painful eye.
And now on foot the frowning warriors light,
And with their ponderous fists renew the fight;
Blow answers blow, their cheeks are smear'd with blood,
Till down they fall, and grappling roll in mud.
So when two boars, in wild Ytene[1] bred,
Or on Westphalia's fattening chesnuts fed,
Gnash their sharp tusks, and, rouz'd with equal fire,
Dispute the reign of some luxurious mire;
In the black flood they wallow o'er and o'er,
Till their arm'd jaws distil with foam and gore.
  Where the mob gathers, swiftly shoot along,
Nor idly mingle in the noisy throng:
Lur'd by the silver hilt, amid the swarm,
The subtle artist will thy side disarm.
Nor is the flaxen wig with safety worn;
High on the shoulder, in a basket borne,
Lurks the sly boy, whose hand, to rapine bred,
Plucks off the curling honours of thy head.
Here dives the skulking thief, with practis'd sleight,
And unfelt fingers make thy pocket light.
Where's now the watch, with all its trinkets, flown?
And thy late snuff-box is no more thy own.
But lo! his bolder thefts some tradesman spies,
Swift from his prey the scudding lurcher flies;
Dext'rous he 'scapes the coach with nimble bounds,
Whilst every honest tongue "Stop thief!" resounds.
So speeds the wily fox, alarm'd by fear,
Who lately filch'd the turkey's callow care;
Hounds following hounds grow louder as he flies,
And injur'd tenants join the hunter's cries.
Breathless, he stumbling falls. Ill-fated boy!
Why did not honest work thy youth employ?
Seiz'd by rough hands, he's dragged amid the rout,
And stretch'd beneath the pump's incessant spout:
Or, plung'd in miry ponds, he gasping lies,
Mud chokes his mouth, and plaisters o'er his eyes.
  Let not the ballad singer's shrilling strain
Amid the swarm thy listening ear detain:
Guard well thy pocket; for these Syrens stand

---

[1] New Forest in Hampshire, anciently so called.

To aid the labours of the diving hand;
Confederate in the cheat, they draw the throng,
And cambric handkerchiefs reward the song.
But soon as coach or cart drives rattling on,
The rabble part, in shoals they backward run.
So Jove's loud bolts the mingled war divide,
And Greece and Troy retreat on either side.

    If the rude throng pour on with furious pace,
And hap to break thee from a friend's embrace,
Stop short; nor struggle through the crowd in vain,
But watch with careful eye the passing train.
Yet I (perhaps too fond), if chance the tide
Tumultuous bear my partner from my side,
Impatient venture back; despising harm,
I force my passage where the thickest swarm.
Thus his lost bride the Trojan sought in vain
Through night, and arms, and flames, and hills of slain.
Thus Nisus wander'd o'er the pathless grove
To find the brave companion of his love.
The pathless grove in vain he wanders o'er:
Euryalus, alas! is now no more.

    That walker who, regardless of his pace,
Turns oft to pore upon the damsel's face,
From side to side by thrusting elbows tost,
Shall strike his aching breast against a post;
Or water, dash'd from fishy stalls, shall stain
His hapless coat with spirts of scaly rain.
But, if unwarily he chance to stray
Where twirling turnstiles intercept the way,
The thwarting passenger shall force them round
And beat the wretch half breathless to the ground.

    Let constant vigilance thy footsteps guide,
And wary circumspection guard thy side;
Then shalt thou walk, unharm'd, the dangerous night,
Nor need th' officious linkboy's smoky light.
Thou never will attempt to cross the road,
Where ale-house benches rest the porter's load,
Grievous to heedless shins; no barrow's wheel,
That bruises oft the truant school-boy's heel,
Behind thee rolling, with insidious pace,
Shall mark thy stocking with a miry trace.
Let not thy venturous steps approach too nigh,
Where, gaping wide, low steepy cellars lie.
Should thy shoe wrench aside, down, down you fall,

And overturn the scolding huckster's stall;
The scolding huckster shall not o'er thee moan,
But pence exact for nuts and pears o'erthrown.
    Though you through cleanlier allies wind by day,
To shun the hurries of the public way,
Yet ne'er to those dark paths by night retire;
Mind only safety, and contemn the mire.
Then no impervious courts thy haste detain,
Nor sneering alewives bid thee turn again.
    Where Lincoln's-inn, wide space, is rail'd around,
Cross not with venturous step; there oft is found
The lurking thief, who, while the day-light shone,
Made the walls echo with his begging tone:
That crutch, which late compassion mov'd, shall wound
Thy bleeding head, and fell thee to the ground.
    Though thou art tempted by the link-man's call,
Yet trust him not along the lonely wall;
In the mid way he'll quench the flaming brand,
And share the booty with the pilfering band.
Still keep the public streets, where oily rays,
Shot from the crystal-lamp o'erspread the ways.

JOHN GAY
(1688-1732).

SALLY IN OUR ALLEY

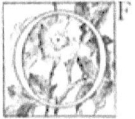

OF all the girls that are so smart
   There's none like pretty Sally;
She is the darling of my heart,
   And she lives in our alley.
There is no lady in the land
   Is half so sweet as Sally;
She is the darling of my heart,
   And she lives in our alley.

Her father he makes cabbage-nets
   And through the streets does cry 'em;
Her mother she sells laces long
   To such as please to buy 'em:
But sure such folks could ne'er beget
   So sweet a girl as Sally!
She is the darling of my heart,
   And she lives in our alley.

When she is by, I leave my work,
   I love her so sincerely;
My master comes like any Turk,
   And bangs me most severely—
But let him bang his bellyful,
   I'll bear it all for Sally;
She is the darling of my heart,
   And she lives in our alley.

Of all the days that's in the week
   I dearly love but one day—
And that's the day that comes betwixt
   A Saturday and Monday;

For then I'm drest all in my best
    To walk abroad with Sally ;
She is the darling of my heart,
    And she lives in our alley.

My master carries me to church,
    And often am I blamed
Because I leave him in the lurch
    As soon as text is named ;
I leave the church in sermon-time
    And slink away to Sally ;
She is the darling of my heart,
    And she lives in our alley.

When Christmas comes about again
    O then I shall have money ;
I'll hoard it up, and box it all,
    I'll give it to my honey:
I would it were ten thousand pound,
    I'd give it all to Sally ;
She is the darling of my heart,
    And she lives in our alley.

My master and the neighbours all
    Make game of me and Sally,
And, but for her, I'd better be
    A slave and row a galley ;
But when my seven long years are out
    O then I'll marry Sally,—
And then how happily we'll live—
    But not in our alley !

HENRY CAREY
(16—,-1743).

ST. JAMES'S CHAPEL

LAST Sunday at St. James's prayers,
    The prince and princess by,
I, drest in all my whale-bone airs,
    Sat in a closet nigh.
I bow'd my knees, I held my book,
    Read all the answers o'er;
But was perverted by a look,
    Which pierced me from the door.
High thoughts of Heaven I came to use
    With the devoutest care;
Which gay young Strephon made me lose,
    And all the raptures there.
He stood to hand me to my chair,
    And bow'd with courtly grace;
But whisper'd love into my ear,
    Too warm for that grave place.
"Love, love," said he, "by all adored,
    My tender heart has won."
But I grew peevish at the word,
    And bade he would be gone.
He went quite out of sight, while I
    A kinder answer meant;
Nor did I for my sins that day
    By half so much repent.

                      ANONYMOUS.

FROM RICHMOND HILL

(1727)

                    SAY, shall we wind
ALONG the streams? or walk the smiling mead?
Or court the forest glades? or wander wild
Among the waving harvests? or ascend,
While radiant Summer opens all its pride,
Thy hill, delightful Shene?[1]   Here let us sweep
The boundless landscape: now the raptured eye,
Exulting, swift to huge Augusta send,
Now to the Sister Hills that skirt her plain,
To lofty Harrow now, and now to where
Majestic Windsor lifts his princely brow.
In lovely contrast to this glorious view
Calmly magnificent, then will we turn
To where the silver Thames first rural grows.
There let the feasted eye unwearied stray:
Luxurious, there, rove through the pendent woods
That nodding hang o'er Harrington's retreat;
And, stopping thence to Ham's embowering walks,
Beneath whose shades, in spotless peace retired,
With her the pleasing partner of his heart,
The worthy Queensberry yet laments his Gay,
And polished Cornbury wooes the willing Muse,
Slow let us trace the matchless vale of Thames;
Fair winding up to where the Muses haunt
In Twit'nam's bowers, and for their Pope implore
The healing God, to royal Hampton's pile,
To Clermont's terraced height, and Esher's groves,
Where in the sweetest solitude, embraced

[1] Ancient name of Richmond.

By the soft windings of the silent Mole,
From courts and senates Pelham finds repose.
Enchanting vale ! beyond whate'er the Muse
Has of Achaia or Hesperia sung !
O vale of bliss ! O softly swelling hills !
On which the power of cultivation lies,
And joys to see the wonders of his toil.
   Heavens ! what a goodly prospect spreads around,
Of hills, and dales, and woods, and lawns, and spires,
And glittering towns, and gilded streams, till all
The stretching landscape into smoke decays !
Happy Britannia ! where the Queen of Arts,
Inspiring vigour, Liberty abroad
Walks, unconfined, even to thy farthest cots,
And scatters plenty with unsparing hand.

JAMES THOMSON
(1700-1748).

LONDON JAUNTS

SO when some City wife for change of air
To Hampstead or to Highgate does repair,
Her to make haste her husband does implore,
And cries, " My dear, the coach is at the door ! "
With equal haste, desirous to be gone,
She gets into the coach, and then she cries, " Drive on ! "

HENRY FIELDING
(1707-1754).

LONDON JARS

SO, when two dogs are fighting in the streets,
    With a third dog one of these two dogs meets;
    With angry tooth he bites him to the bone
    And *this* dog smarts for what *that* dog hath done!

HENRY FIELDING.

THE RED LION, HENLEY

To thee, fair Freedom! I retire,
    From flattery, feasting, dice and din;
Nor art thou found in domes much higher
    Than the lone cot or humble Inn.

'Tis here with boundless power I reign,
    And every health which I begin,
Converts dull port to bright champagne;
    For Freedom crowns it, at an Inn.

I fly from pomp, I fly from state,
    I fly from falsehood's spacious grin;
Freedom I love, and form I hate,
    And choose my lodgings at an Inn.

Here, waiter! take my sordid ore,
    Which lacqueys else might hope to win;
It buys what Courts have not in store,
    It buys me Freedom, at an Inn.

And now once more I shape my way
    Through rain or shine, through thick or thin,
Secure to meet, at close of day,
    With kind reception at an Inn.

Whoe'er has travell'd life's dull round,
    Where'er his stages may have been,
May sigh to think how oft he found
    The warmest welcome—at an Inn.

                WILLIAM SHENSTONE
                    (1714-1763).

ODE ON A DISTANT PROSPECT OF ETON COLLEGE

(1742)

YE distant spires, ye antique towers,
   That crown the watery glade,
Where grateful Science still adores
   Her Henry's holy shade ;
And ye, that from the stately brow
Of Windsor's heights the expanse below
   Of grove, of lawn, of mead, survey,
Whose turf, whose shade, whose flowers among
Wanders the hoary Thames along
   His silver-winding way :

Ah, happy hills ! ah, pleasing shade !
   Ah, fields beloved in vain !
Where once my careless childhood strayed,
   A stranger yet to pain !
I feel the gales that from ye blow
A momentary bliss bestow,
   As waving fresh their gladsome wing,
My weary soul they seem to soothe,
And, redolent of joy and youth,
   To breathe a second spring.

Say, Father Thames, for thou hast seen
   Full many a sprightly race
Disporting on thy margent green,
   The paths of pleasure trace ;
Who foremost now delight to cleave,
With pliant arm, thy glassy wave ?
   The captive linnet which enthrall ?

What idle progeny succeed
To chase the rolling circle's speed,
  Or urge the flying ball ?

While some, on earnest business bent,
  Their murmuring labours ply
'Gainst graver hours that bring constraint
  To sweeten liberty,
Some bold adventurers disdain
The limits of their little reign,
  And unknown regions dare descry :
Still as they run they look behind,
They hear a voice in every wind,
  And snatch a fearful joy.

Gay hope is theirs, by fancy fed,
  Less pleasing when possest ;
The tear forgot as soon as shed,
  The sunshine of the breast :
Theirs buxom health of rosy hue,
Wild wit, invention ever new,
  And lively cheer, of vigour born ;
The thoughtless day, the easy night,
The spirits pure, the slumbers light,
  That fly the approach of morn.

Alas ! regardless of their doom,
  The little victims play ;
No sense have they of ills to come,
  Nor care beyond to-day :
Yet see how all around them wait
The ministers of human fate,
  And black Misfortune's baleful train !
Ah, show them where in ambush stand,
To seize their prey, the murtherous band !
  Ah, tell them they are men !

These shall the fury passions tear,
  The vultures of the mind,—
Disdainful Anger, pallid Fear,
  And Shame that skulks behind ;
Or pining Love shall waste their youth,
Or Jealousy, with rankling tooth,
  That inly gnaws the secret heart ;

And Envy wan and faded Care,
Grim-visaged comfortless Despair,
   And Sorrow's piercing dart.

Ambition this will tempt to rise,
   Then whirl the wretch from high,
To bitter Scorn a sacrifice,
   And grinning Infamy.
The stings of Falsehood those shall try,
And hard Unkindness' altered eye,
   That mocks the tear it forced to flow ;
And keen Remorse with blood defiled,
And moody Madness laughing wild
   Amid severest woe.

Lo ! in the vale of years beneath
   A grisly troop are seen,
The painful family of Death,
   More hideous than their queen :
This racks the joints, this fires the veins,
That every labouring sinew strains,
   Those in the deeper vitals rage ;
Lo ! Poverty, to fill the band,
That numbs the soul with icy hand,
   And slow-consuming Age.

To each his sufferings : all are men,
   Condemned alike to groan ;
The tender for another's pain,
   The unfeeling for his own.
Yet, ah ! why should they know their fate,
Since sorrow never comes too late,
   And happiness too swiftly flies ?
Thought would destroy their paradise.
No more ;—where ignorance is bliss,
   'Tis folly to be wise.

THOMAS GRAY
(1716-1771).

STRAWBERRY-HILL

A Ballad

tune of a former song written by G. Bubb Doddington, Lord Melcomb, *the burthen of which was,* My Strawberry, my Strawberry shall bear away the Bell.

I

"Some cry up Gunnersbury,[1]
 For Sion some declare;
And some say that with Chiswick-house[2]
 No villa can compare:
But ask the beaux of Middlesex,
 Who know the county well,
If Strawb'ry-hill, if Strawb'ry-hill
 Don't bear away the bell?

II

"Some love to roll down Greenwich-hill
 For this thing and for that;
And some prefer sweet Marble-hill,[3]
 Tho' sure 'tis somewhat flat:
Yet Marble-hill and Greenwich-hill,
 If Kitty Clive can tell,
From Strawb'ry-hill, from Strawb'ry-hill
 Will never bear the bell.

III

"Tho' Surrey boasts its Oatlands,[4]
 And Clermont[5] kept so jim [neat],

---

[1] Where lived the Princess Amelia, now, in a re-erected form, Lord Rothschild's.
[2] Now the Marquis of Bute's, at Chiswick.   [3] Lady Suffolk's.
[4] Duke of York's, near Weybridge.   [5] Claremont, the Duke of Newcastle's, at Esher.

And some prefer sweet Southcote's,[1]
    'Tis but a dainty whim :
For ask the gallant Bristow,
    Who does in taste excell,
If Strawb'ry-hill, if Strawb'ry-hill
    Don't bear away the bell?

IV

" Since Denham sung of Cooper's,
    There's scarce a hill around,
But what in song or ditty
    Is turn'd to fairy-ground—
Ah ! peace be with their memories !
    I wish them wond'rous well,
But Strawb'ry-hill, but Strawb'ry-hill
    Must bear away the bell.

V

" Great William dwells at Windsor,[2]
    As Edward did of old,
And many a Gaul and many a Scot
    Have found him full as bold.
On lofty hills like Windsor
    Such heroes ought to dwell,
Yet little folks like Strawb'ry-hill,
    Like Strawb'ry-hill as well."

[1] Philip Southcote's *ferme ornée* at Woburn Park.
[2] Cumberland Lodge, at the end of the Long Walk at Windsor.

(*N.B.*—This is copied from Walpole's *Catalogue of Strawberry Hill*, 1774, pp. 117-119. A not
" The 2nd, 4th, and 5th stanzas were added by another hand " [*i.e.* Walpole's own].)

WILLIAM PULTENEY, EARL OF BATH
(1682-1764).

A CHAMBER IN GRUB STREET

HERE the Red Lion, staring o'er the way,
Invites each passing stranger that can pay ;
Where Calvert's butt and Parsons' black champai
Regale the drabs and bloods of Drury Lane ;
There in a lonely room, from bailiff's snug,
The Muse found Scroggen stretched beneath a rug ;
A window, patched with paper, lent a ray
That dimly showed the state in which he lay ;
The sanded floor, that grits beneath the tread ;
The humid wall with paltry pictures spread ;
The royal game of goose was there in view,
And the twelve rules the Royal Martyr drew ;
The *Seasons*, framed with listing, found a place,
And brave Prince William show'd his lampblack face :
The morn was cold ; he views with keen desire
The rusty grate unconscious of a fire :
With beer and milk arrears the frieze was scored,
And five crack'd teacups drap'd the chimney-board ;
A nightcap deck'd his brows instead of bay ;
A cap by night—a stocking all the day !

OLIVER GOLDSMITH
(1728-1774).

THE CONTRAST

N London I never knew what I'd be at,
Enraptured with this, and enchanted with that;
I'm wild with the sweets of variety's plan,
And Life seems a blessing too happy for man.

But the Country, Lord help me! sets all matters right,
So calm and composing from morning to night;
Oh! it settles the spirits when nothing is seen
But an ass on a common, a goose on a green.

In town, if it rain, why it damps not our hope,
The eye has her choice, and the fancy her scope;
What harm though it pour whole nights or whole days?
It spoils not our prospects, or stops not our ways.

In the country what bliss, when it rains in the fields,
To live on the transports that shuttlecock yields;
Or go crawling from window to window, to see
A pig on a dunghill, or crow on a tree.

In London, if folks ill together are put,
A bore may be dropt, and a quiz may be cut;
We change without end; and if lazy or ill,
All wants are at hand, and all wishes at will.

In the country you're nail'd, like a pale in the park,
To some *stick* of a neighbour that's cramm'd in the ark;
And 'tis odd, if you're hurt, or in fits tumble down,
You reach death ere the doctor can reach you from town.

A LONDON GARLAND

In London how easy we visit and meet,
Gay pleasure's the theme, and sweet smiles are our treat:
Our morning's a round of good-humour'd delight,
And we rattle, in comfort, to pleasure at night.

In the country, how sprightly! our visits we make
Through ten miles of mud, for Formality's sake;
With the coachman in drink, and the moon in a fog,
And no thought in our head but a ditch or a bog.

In London the spirits are cheerful and light,
All places are gay and all faces are bright;
We've ever new joys, and revived by each whim,
Each day on a fresh tide of pleasure we swim.

But how gay in the country! what summer delight
To be waiting for winter from morning to night!
Then the fret of impatience gives exquisite glee
To relish the sweet rural subjects we see.

In town we've no use for the skies overhead,
For when the sun rises then we go to bed;
And as to that old-fashion'd virgin the moon,
She shines out of season, like satin in June.

In the country these planets delightfully glare
Just to show us the object we want isn't there;
O, how cheering and gay, when their beauties arise,
To sit and gaze round with the tears in one's eyes!

But 'tis in the country alone we can find
That happy resource, that relief to the mind,
When, drove to despair, our last efforts we make,
And drag the old fish-pond, for novelty's sake.

Indeed I must own 'tis a pleasure complete
To see ladies well draggled and wet in their feet,
But what is all that to the transport we feel
When we capture, in triumph, two toads and an eel!

I have heard tho' that love in a cottage is sweet,
When two hearts in one link of soft sympathy meet
That's to come—for as yet I, alas! am a swain
Who require, I own it, more links to my chain.

A LONDON GARLAND

Your magpies and stock-doves may flirt among trees,
And chatter their transports in groves, if they please:
But a house is much more to my taste than a tree,
And for groves, O! a good grove of chimneys for me.

In the country, if Cupid should find a man out,
The poor tortured victim mopes hopeless about;
But in London, thank Heaven! our peace is secure,
Where, for one eye to kill, there's a thousand to cure.

I know love's a devil, too subtle to spy,
That shoots through the soul, from the beam of an eye;
But in London these devils so quick fly about,
That a new devil still drives an old devil out.

In town let me live then, in town let me die,
For in truth I can't relish the country, not I.
If one must have a villa in summer to dwell,
O, give me the sweet shady side of Pall Mall!

CAPTAIN CHARLES MORRIS

(1740-1832).

WAPPING OLD STAIRS

YOUR Molly has never been false, she declares,
   Since the last time we parted at Wapping Old Stairs;
   When I said that I would continue the same,
   And gave you the 'bacco box mark'd with my name.
When I passed a whole fortnight between decks with you,
Did I e'er give a kiss, Tom, to one of your crew?
To be useful and kind to my Thomas I stay'd,
For his trousers I wash'd, and his grog too I made.

Though you promised last Sunday to walk in the Mall
With Susan from Deptford and likewise with Sall,
In silence I stood your unkindness to hear,
And only upbraided my Tom with a tear.
Why should Sall, or should Susan, than me be more prized?
For the heart that is true, Tom, should ne'er be despised.
Then be constant and kind, nor your Molly forsake;
Still your trousers I'll wash, and your grog too I'll make.

                        CHARLES DIBDIN
                           (1745-1814).

HOLY THURSDAY

'TWAS on a Holy Thursday, their innocent faces clean,
Came children walking two and two, in red, and blue, and green :
Grey-headed beadles walk'd before, with wands as white as snow,
Till into the high dome of St. Paul's, they like Thames' waters flow.

O what a multitude they seem'd, these flowers of London town,
Seated in companies they were, with radiance all their own :
The hum of multitudes was there, but multitudes of lambs,
Thousands of little boys and girls raising their innocent hands.

Now like a mighty wind they raise to heaven the voice of song,
Or like harmonious thunderings the seats of heaven among :
Beneath them sit the aged men, wise guardians of the poor.
Then cherish pity, lest you drive an angel from your door.

WILLIAM BLAKE
(1757-1827).

LONDON FROM SHOOTER'S HILL

THE sun went down, the smoke rose up, as from
A half-unquench'd volcano, o'er a space
Which well beseem'd the "Devil's drawing-room,"
As some have qualified that wondrous place:
But Juan felt, though not approaching *home*,
As one who, though he were not of the race,
Revered the soil, of those true sons the mother,
Who butcher'd half the earth, and bullied t'other.

A mighty mass of brick, and smoke, and shipping,
Dirty and dusky, but as wide as eye
Could reach, with here and there a sail just skipping
In sight, then lost amidst the forestry
Of masts; a wilderness of steeples peeping
On tiptoe through their sea-coal canopy;
A huge, dun cupola, like a foolscap crown
On a fool's head—and there is London Town!

But Juan saw not this: each wreath of smoke
Appear'd to him but as the magic vapour
Of some alchymic furnace, from whence broke
The wealth of worlds (a wealth of tax and paper):
The gloomy clouds, which o'er it as a yoke
Are bow'd, and put the sun out like a taper,
Were nothing but the natural atmosphere,
Extremely wholesome, though but rarely clear.

GEORGE GORDON BYRON, LORD BYRON
(1788-1824).

UPON WESTMINSTER BRIDGE

Sept. 3, 1802

EARTH has not anything to show more fair :
Dull would he be of soul who could pass by
A sight so touching in its majesty :
This City now doth like a garment wear

The beauty of the morning : silent, bare,
Ships, towers, domes, theatres, and temples lie
Open unto the fields, and to the sky,—
All bright and glittering in the smokeless air.

Never did sun more beautifully steep
In his first splendour valley, rock, or hill ;
Ne'er saw I, never felt, a calm so deep !

The river glideth at his own sweet will :
Dear God ! the very houses seem asleep ;
And all that mighty heart is lying still !

WILLIAM WORDSWORTH
(1770-1850).

THE MERMAID TAVERN

SOULS of poets dead and gone,
    What Elysium have ye known,
    Happy field or mossy cavern,
    Choicer than the Mermaid Tavern?
    Have ye tippled drink more fine
Than mine host's Canary wine?
Or are fruits of Paradise
Sweeter than those dainty pies
Of venison? O generous food!
Drest as though bold Robin Hood
Would, with his maid Marian,
Sup and browse from horn and can.

  I have heard that on a day
Mine host's sign-board flew away,
Nobody knew whither, till
An astrologer's old quill
To a sheepskin gave the story,—
Said he saw you in your glory,
Underneath a new old-sign
Sipping beverage divine,
And pledging with contented smack
The Mermaid in the Zodiac.

  Souls of poets dead and gone,
What Elysium have ye known,
Happy field or mossy cavern,
Choicer than the Mermaid Tavern?

                        JOHN KEATS
                        (1795-1821).

MOLESEY HURST

'IS Life to see the first dawn stain
With sallow light the window pane:
To dress—to wear a rough drab coat,
With large pearl buttons all afloat
Upon the waves of plush: to tie
A kerchief of the king-cup dye
(White-spotted with a small bird's-eye)
Around the neck, and from the nape
Let fall an easy, fan-like cape!
'Tis Life to reach the livery stable,
Secure the *ribbands* and the *day-bill*,
And mount a gig that had a spring
Some summers back, and then take wing
Behind (in Mr. Hamlet's tongue)
A guide whose " withers are unwrung ";
Who stands erect, and yet forlorn,
And, from a *half-pay* life of corn,
Showing as many points each way
As Martial's " Epigrammata ";
Yet who, when set a-going goes
Like one undestined to repose.
'Tis LIFE to revel down the road,
And *queer* each o'erfraught chaise's load;
To rave and rattle at the *gate*,
And shower upon the *gatherer's* pate
Oaths by the dozen, and such speeches
As well betoken one's *slang* riches;
To take of Deady's bright *stark-naked*
A glass or so—'tis LIFE to take it!
O, it is LIFE to see a proud
And dauntless man step, full of hopes,
Up to the P.C. stakes and ropes,

A LONDON GARLAND

Throw in his hat, and, with a spring,
Get gallantly within the Ring ;
Eye the wide crowd, and walk awhile,
Taking all cheering with a smile !
To watch him strip his well-trained form,
White, glowing, muscular, and warm,
All beautiful and conscious power
Released and quiet till the hour :
His glossy and transparent frame
In radiant plight to strive for fame !
To look upon the clean-shaped limb
In silk and flannel clothéd trim ;
While round the waist the kerchief tied
Makes the flesh glow in richer pride !
'Tis more than LIFE to watch him hold
His hand forth, tremulous yet bold,
Over his second's, and to clasp
His rival's in a quiet grasp ;
To watch the noble attitude
He takes—the crowd in breathless mood ;
And then to see with adamant start
The muscles set, and the great heart
Throb a courageous, splendid light
Into the eyes—and then—THE FIGHT !

JOHN HAMILTON REYNOLDS
(1795-1852 ?).

THE BOY AT THE NORE

SAY, little Boy at the Nore,
   Do you come from the small Isle of Man?
Why, your history a mystery must be,—
   Come tell us as much as you can,
        Little Boy at the Nore!

You live, it seems, wholly on water,
   Which your Gambier calls living in clover;
But how comes it, if that is the case,
   You're eternally half-seas over,—
        Little Boy at the Nore?

While you ride, while you dance, while you float,—
   Never mind your imperfect orthography;
But give us, as well as you can,
   Your watery autobiography,
        Little Boy at the Nore!

      BOY AT THE NORE *loquitur*

I'm the tight little Boy at the Nore,
   In a sort of sea negus I dwells;
Half and half 'twixt salt-water and Port,
   I'm reckoned the first of the swells,—
        I'm the Boy at the Nore!

I lives with my toes to the flounders,
   And watches through long days and nights;
Yet, cruelly eager, men look
   To catch the first glimpse of my lights,—
        I'm the Boy at the Nore.

I never gets cold in the head,
  So my life on salt water is sweet ;
I think I owes much of my health
  To being well used to wet feet—
    As the Boy at the Nore.

There's one thing, I'm never in debt ;
  Nay !—I liquidates more than I oughter ;
So the man to beat Cits as goes by,
  In keeping the head above water,
    Is the Boy at the Nore.

I've seen a good deal of distress,
  Lots of Breakers in Ocean's Gazette ;
They should do as I do,—rise o'er all ;
  Ay, a good floating capital get,
    Like the boy at the Nore !

I'm a'ter the sailor's own heart,
  And cheers him, in deep water rolling ;
And the friend of all friends to Jack Junk,
  Ben Backstay, Tom Pipes, and Tom Bowling,
    Is the Boy at the Nore !

Could I e'er but grow up, I'd be off
  For a week to make love to my wheedles ;
If the tight little Boy at the Nore
  Could but catch a nice girl at the Needles,
    We'd have two at the Nore !

They thinks little of sizes on water,
  On big waves the tiny one skulks,—
While the river has Men of War on it,—
  Yes, the Thames is oppressed with Great Hulks,
    And the Boy's at the Nore !

But I've done,—for the water is heaving
  Round my body as though it would sink it !
And I've been so long pitching and tossing,
  That sea-sick—you'd hardly now think it—
    Is the Boy at the Nore !

THOMAS HOOD
(1798-1845).

A BALLAD OF GUY FAWKES

I

SING a doleful tragedy,
    Guy Fawkes the prince of sinisters,
Who once blew up the House of Lords,
    The King and all his Ministers ;
    That is—he would have blown them up,
And folks will ne'er forget him ;
His will was good to do the deed—
    That is—if they'd have let him—
        Bow, wow, wow,
        Right tol de riddle diddle,
        Bow, wow, wow.

II

He straightway came from Lambeth side,
    And wish'd the state was undone ;
And, crossing over Vauxhall Bridge,
    That way came into London ;
That is—he would have come that way
    To perpetrate his guilt, Sirs ;
But a little thing prevented him ;—
    The bridge it was not built, Sirs.

III

Then searching through the dreary vaults,
    With portable gas-light, Sirs,
About to touch the powder train,
    At witching hour of night, Sirs—

That is—he would have used the gas,
　　But that he was prevented ;
Because, you see, in James's time
　　It had not been invented.

IV

And when they caught him in the fact,
　　So very near the Crown's end,
They straightway sent to Bow Street,
　　For the famous runner Townsend ;
That is—they would have sent for him,
　　For fear he was no starter at—
But Townsend was not living then ;
　　He wasn't born till *arter* that.

V

So then they put poor Guy to death,
　　For ages to remember,
And boys now *burn* him, once a year,
　　In dreary, dark November ;
That is—I mean his effigy,
　　For truth is strong and steady—
Poor Guy they cannot kill again,
　　Because he's dead already.

VI

Then bless Her Gracious Majesty
　　And bless her Royal Son, Sirs,
And may he never get blown up :
　　We can't spare such a one, Sirs.
And if he's King, I'm sure he'll reign—
　　So prophesies my song, Sirs,
But if he don't, why then he won't,
　　And so I can't be wrong, Sirs.

　　　　　　　　　　THOMAS HUDSON.

GOOD NIGHT TO THE SEASON

GOOD night to the Season! 'Tis over!
 Gay dwellings no longer are gay;
The courtier, the gambler, the lover,
 Are scattered like swallows away.
There's nobody left to invite one
 Except my good uncle and spouse;
My mistress is bathing at Brighton,
 My patron is sailing at Cowes;
For want of better employment,
 Till Ponto and Don can get out,
I'll cultivate rural enjoyment,
 And angle immensely for trout.

Good night to the Season!—the lobbies,
 Their changes and rumours of change,
Which startled the rustic Sir Bobbies,
 And made all the Bishops look strange;
The breaches, and battles, and blunders,
 Performed by the Commons and Peers;
The Marquis's eloquent blunders,
 The Baronet's eloquent ears;
Denouncings of Papists and treasons,
 Of foreign dominions and oats;
Misrepresentations of reasons,
 And misunderstandings of notes.

Good night to the Season!—the buildings
 Enough to make Inigo sick;
The paintings, and plasterings, and gildings
 Of stucco, and marble, and brick:
The orders deliciously blended
 From love of effect into one;

The club-houses only intended,
   The palaces only begun ;
The hell, where the fiend in his glory
   Sits staring at putty and stones,
And scrambles from story to story,
   To rattle at midnight his bones.

Good night to the Season !—the dances,
   The fillings of hot little rooms,
The glancings of rapturous glances,
   The fancyings of fancy costumes ;
The pleasures which fashion makes duties,
   The praisings of fiddles and flutes,
The luxury of looking at Beauties,
   The tedium of talking to mutes ;
The female diplomatists, planners
   Of matches for Laura and Jane ;
The ice of her Ladyship's manners,
   The ice of his Lordship's champagne.

Good night to the Season !—the rages
   Led off by the chiefs of the throng,
The Lady Matilda's new pages,
   The Lady Eliza's new song ;
Miss Fennel's macaw, which at Boodle's
   Was held to have something to say ;
Mr. Splenetic's musical poodles
   Which bark " *Batti Batti*" all day ;
The pony Sir Araby sported,
   As hot and as black as a coal,
And the Lion his mother imported,
   In bearskins and grease, from the Pole.

Good night to the Season !—the Toso,
   So very majestic and tall ;
Miss Ayton, whose singing was so-so,
   And Pasta, divinest of all ;
The labour in vain of the ballet,
   So sadly deficient in stars ;
The foreigners thronging the Alley,
   Exhaling the breath of cigars ;
The *loge* where some heiress (how killing !)
   Environed with exquisites sits,
The lovely one out of her drilling,
   The silly ones out of their wits.

Good night to the Season !—the splendour
   That beamed in the Spanish Bazaar ;
Where I purchased—my heart was so tender—
   A card-case, a pasteboard guitar,
A bottle of perfume, a girdle,
   A lithographed Riego, full-grown,
Whom bigotry drew on a hurdle
   That artists might draw him on stone ;
A small panorama of Seville,
   A trap for demolishing flies,
A caricature of the Devil,
   And a look from Miss Sheridan's eyes.

Good night to the Season !—the flowers
   Of the grand horticultural fête,
When boudoirs were quitted for bowers,
   And the fashion was—not to be late ;
When all who had money and leisure
   Grew rural o'er ices and wines,
All pleasantly toiling for pleasure,
   All hungrily pining for pines,
And making of beautiful speeches,
   And marring of beautiful shows,
And feeding on delicate peaches,
   And treading on delicate toes.

Good night to the Season !—Another
   Will come with its trifles and toys,
And hurry away, like its brother,
   In sunshine, and odour, and noise.
Will it come with a rose or a briar ?
   Will it come with a blessing or curse ?
Will its bonnets be lower or higher?
   Will its morals be better or worse?
Will it find me grown thinner or fatter,
   Or fonder of wrong or of right,
Or married—or buried ?—no matter :
   Good night to the Season—good night !

                WINTHROP MACKWORTH PRAED
                        (1802-1839).

I

THAT 'twere possible
After long grief and pain
To find the arms of my true love
Round me once again!

II

When I was wont to meet her
In the silent woody places
By the home that gave me birth,
We stood tranced in long embraces
Mixt with kisses sweeter sweeter
Than anything on earth.

III

A shadow flits before me,
Not thou, but like to thee:
Ah Christ, that it were possible
For one short hour to see
The souls we loved, that they might tell us
What and where they be.

IV

It leads me forth at evening,
It lightly winds and steals
In a cold white robe before me,
When all my spirit reels
At the shouts, the leagues of lights,
And the roaring of the wheels.

A LONDON GARLAND

V

Half the night I waste in sighs,
Half in dreams I sorrow after
The delight of early skies;
In a wakeful doze I sorrow
For the hand, the lips, the eyes,
For the meeting of the morrow,
The delight of happy laughter,
The delight of low replies.

VI

'Tis a morning pure and sweet,
And a dewy splendour falls
On the little flower that clings
To the turrets and the walls;
'Tis a morning pure and sweet,
And the light and shadow fleet;
She is walking in the meadow,
And the woodland echo rings;
In a moment we shall meet;
She is singing in the meadow
And the rivulet at her feet
Ripples on in light and shadow
To the ballad that she sings.

VII

Do I hear her sing as of old,
My bird with the shining head,
My own dove with the tender eye?
But there rings on a sudden a passionate cry,
There is some one dying or dead,
And a sullen thunder is roll'd;
For a tumult shakes the city,
And I wake, my dream is fled;
In the shuddering dawn, behold,
Without knowledge, without pity,
By the curtains of my bed
That abiding phantom cold.

VIII

Get thee hence, nor come again,
Mix not memory with doubt,
Pass, thou deathlike type of pain,
Pass and cease to move about!
'Tis the blot upon the brain
That *will* show itself without.

IX

Then I rise, the eavedrops fall,
And the yellow vapours choke
The great city sounding wide;
The day comes, a dull red ball
Wrapt in drifts of lurid smoke
On the misty river-tide.

X

Thro' the hubbub of the market
I steal, a wasted frame,
It crosses here, it crosses there,
Thro' all that crowd confused and loud,
The shadow still the same;
And on my heavy eyelids
My anguish hangs like shame.

XI

Alas for her that met me,
That heard me softly call,
Came glimmering thro' the laurels
At the quiet evenfall,
In the garden by the turrets
Of the old manorial hall.

XII

Would the happy spirit descend,
From the realms of light and song,
In the chamber or the street,
As she looks among the blest,
Should I fear to greet my friend
Or to say, "Forgive the wrong,"
Or to ask her, "Take me, sweet,
To the regions of thy rest"?

XIII

But the broad light glares and beats,
And the shadow flits and fleets
And will not let me be;
And I loathe the squares and streets,
And the faces that one meets,
Hearts with no love for me:
Always I long to creep
Into some still cavern deep,
There to weep, and weep, and weep
My whole soul out to thee.

ALFRED TENNYSON
(1809-1892).

THE IDLER

WITH the London hubbub
    Over-tired and pestered,
I sought out a subbub
    Where I lay sequestered—
Where I lay for three days,
    From Saturday till Monday,
And (per face aut neface)
    Made the most of Sunday;

Burning of a *chee*root
    When I'd had a skinful,
Squatting on a tree root,
    Doubting if 'twas sinful;
As the bells of Kingston
    Made a pretty clangour,
I (forgiving heathen)
    Heard them not in anger:—

Heard and rather fancied
    Their reverberations,
As I sat entrancéd
    With my meditations.
From my Maker's praises
    Easily I wandered,
To pull up His daisies,
    As I sat and pondered.

As I pull'd His daisies
    Into little pieces,
Much I thought of life
    And how small its ease is:

A LONDON GARLAND

Much I blamed the world
   For its worldly vanity,
As my smoke upcurl'd,
   Type of its inanity.

By world I meant the Town
   Mayfair, and its high doings;
Or rather my own set,
   Its chatterings and cooings:
So I view'd the strife
   And the sport of London,
Doubting if its life
   Were overdone or undone.

Be it slow or rapid,
   If it wakes or slumbers,
Anyhow it's vapid—
   Moonshine from cucumbers.
Man is useless too,
   Be he saint or satyr;
Nothing's new or true,
   And—it doesn't matter.

May not I and Jeames
   Be compared together,
I in inking reams,
   He in blacking leather?
Snob and swell are peers;
   Snuffer, chewer, whiffer—
In a hundred years
   Wherein shall we differ?

Counting on to-morrow's
   "Oirish." Whither tendeth
He who simply borrows,
   He who simpler lendeth;
If we give or take,
   Where remains the profit?
Sold or wide awake,
   All will go to Tophet.

To Tophet—shady club
   Where no one need propose ye,
Where Hamlet hints "the rub"
   Is not select or cosy.

In that mixed vulgar place,
  It doesn't matter who pays,
There's no more " Bouillabaise "
  And no more *Petits soupers*.

Why then seek to vie
  With Solomons or Sidneys?
Why care for Strasbourg pie,
  For punch or devilled kidneys?
Why write " Yellow Plush " ?
  Why should we *not* wear it?
Wherefore should we blush?
  Rather grin and bear it.

These uprooted daisies
  Speak of useless trouble,
Cheroots that burn like blazes
  Show that life's a bubble.
Thus musing on our lot,
  A fogeyfied old sinner,
I'm glad to say I got—
  An appetite for dinner.

                              ANONYMOUS.

SUMMER IN HYDE PARK

(GLIMPSES)

I

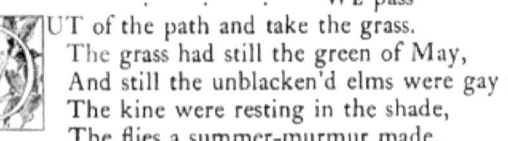

. . . We pass
 out of the path and take the grass.
The grass had still the green of May,
And still the unblacken'd elms were gay;
The kine were resting in the shade,
The flies a summer-murmur made.
Bright was the morn and south the air;
The soft couch'd cattle were as fair
As those which pastured by the sea,
That old-world morn, in Sicily,
When on the beach the Cyclops lay,
And Galatea from the bay
Mock'd her poor love-lorn giant's lay.

. . . . . .
Still we walked on, in thoughtful mood,
And now upon the bridge we stood.
Full of sweet breathings was the air,
Of sudden stirs and pauses fair.
Down o'er the stately Bridge the breeze
Came rustling from the garden-trees
And on the sparkling waters play'd;
Light-plashing waves an answer made,
And mimic boats their haven near'd.
Beyond, the Abbey-towers appear'd
By mist and chimneys unconfined,
Free to the sweep of light and wind;
While through their earth-moor'd nave below
Another breath of wind doth blow,

Sound as of wandering breeze—but sound
In laws by human artists bound.

. . . . .

Onward we moved, and reach'd the Ride
Where gaily flows the human tide.
Afar, in rest the cattle lay ;
We heard, afar, faint music play ;
But agitated, brisk, and near,
Men, with their stream of life, were here.
Some hang upon the rails, and some
On foot behind them go and come.
This through the Ride upon his steed
Goes slowly by, and this at speed.
The young, the happy, and the fair,
The old, the sad, the worn, were there ;
Some vacant, and some musing went,
And some in talk and merriment.
Nods, smiles, and greetings, and farewells !
And now and then, perhaps, there swells
A sigh, a tear—but in the throng
All changes fast, and hies along.
Hies, ah, from whence, what native ground ?
And to what goal, what ending, bound ?

MATTHEW ARNOLD
(1822-1888).

A COVENT GARDEN PASTORAL

YOUNG Colin must quit the fair meadows of Kent
On a trip to Great Britain's gay capital bent;
Brief leisure is Colin's of Daphne to dream,
As he pilots his waggon and whips up his team.
For the lord of young Colin hath acres to farm—
'Tis a trade that is not without merit or charm;—
And he makes it his pride, by all possible means,
To supply the big City with carrots and greens.

The team and the waggon progress through the night
(Until eastward are traces of dawn's ruddy light).—
See, they traverse the Thames, and they traverse the Strand,
And the lamps of the Market at last are at hand.
Then Colin repairs to a tavern hard by—
For the journey was lonesome, and Colin is dry.—
And he thinks, while he drinks of his—never-mind-what,
O'er the memories dear to that classical spot.

" Ah, shades of the wealthy—the gay—the renowned—
Yet again do ye hover this precinct around;
Yet again with emotion your worshipper thrills,
While he watches ye crowding to Button's and Will's.
Our Congreve and Wycherley, Dryden and Pope,
Never more in the flesh to behold can we hope;
Still their spirits are here, 'mid the mart's busy din—
Waiter!—Talking of spirits—a little more gin!

". Not a step from the corner was Garrick's abode—
Kitty Clive had a residence over the road;
Here Churchill has rhymed on his dark second floor,
And the gallants have knocked at Peg Woffington's door.

Harry Fielding's papa, the much-dreaded Sir John,
Was the Midas of Bow Street, a little way on.
What ghosts reappear 'mid the mart's busy hum!—
Waiter!—Keep'st thou the fluid called Pine-apple rum?

" Yon churchyard can boast of remarkable bones,
Though yon church be unworthy of Inigo Jones;
And yon pile at the corner—called Evans's now—
Echoed once the grand accents of Siddons, I trow.
To the deathless departed again let me drink.—
Waiter!—Fill me my goblet once more to the brink.
This libation—the last one—I'll solemnly pour:
Then return to take charge of that waggon and four!"

HENRY S. LEIGH.

THE BELLS OF SAINT MARTIN'S

(Written in Sickness)

LYING as close a captive here
    As Damiens on his bed of steel,
Restless I turn and lend an ear
    To ev'ry fast-revolving wheel.
My spirit would be all unmann'd
    In silent or suburban gloom;—
But in the gay and giddy Strand
    My Cockney soul hath elbow-room.

I cannot walk; I cannot stir—
    Save painfully from side to side.
My fate, should any fire occur,
    Simply consists in getting fried.
I dream by day, and watch by night
    The dancing shadows on the wall.
My couch, though not an Eden quite,
    Is not unpleasant, after all.

On Friday nights at eight o'clock
    Begins my merriest of times:
My cradled slumberings to rock
    Ring out Saint Martin's merry chimes.
My head may throb, my bones may ache:
    But—when those happy bells begin—
I murmur (only half awake),
    "Peace to the soul of Nelly Gwynne!"

The ringers there, across the way,
    Who bid the cheering metal speak,
Receive, as portion of their pay,
    A leg of mutton once a week.

A LONDON GARLAND

Poor Mistress Eleanor, good soul,
    Bequeathed this banquet in her will.
(Although a sinner on the whole,
    With all her faults I love her still.)

I greet with joy (as many must)
    The merry, merry bells of Yule;
And never was averse, I trust,
    From any others as a rule.
But none will ever match the mirth
    My favoured belfry's clangour yields.
Of all the chimes on all the earth
    Give *me* Saint Martin's in the Fields!

                            HENRY S. LEIGH

THE BURDEN OF NINEVEH

N our Museum galleries
    To-day I lingered o'er the prize
    Dead Greece vouchsafes to living eyes,—
    Her Art for ever in fresh wise
    From hour to hour rejoicing me.
Sighing I turned at last to win
Once more the London dirt and din;
And as I made the swing door spin
And issued, they were hoisting in
    A wingèd beast from Nineveh.

A human face the creature wore,
And hoofs behind and hoofs before,
And flanks with dark runes fretted o'er.
'Twas bull, 'twas mitred Minotaur,
    A dead disbowelled mystery:
The mummy of a buried faith
Stark from the charnel without scathe,
Its wings stood for the light to bathe,—
Such fossil cerements as might swathe
    The very corpse of Nineveh.

The print of its first rush-wrapping
Round it ere it dried, still ribbed the thing.
What song did the brown maidens sing,
From purple mouths alternating,
    When that was woven languidly?
What vows, what rites, what prayers preferr'd,
What songs has the strange image heard?
In what blind vigil stood interr'd
For ages, till an English word
    Broke silence first at Nineveh?

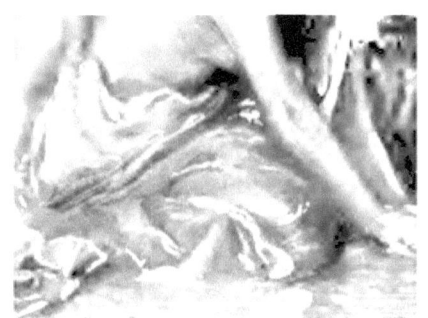

A LONDON GARLAND

Oh when upon each sculptured court,
Where even the wind might not resort,—
O'er which Time passed, of like import
With the wild Arab boys at sport,—
A living face looked in to see:—
Oh seemed it not—the spell once broke—
As though the carven warriors woke,
As though the shaft the string forsook,
The cymbals clashed, the chariots shook,
And there was life in Nineveh?

On London stones our sun anew
The beast's recovered shadow threw.
(No shade that plague of darkness knew,
No light, no shade, while older grew
By ages the old earth and sea.)
Lo thou! could all thy priests have shown
Such proof to make thy godhead known?
From their dead Past thou liv'st alone;
And still thy shadow is thine own,
Even as of yore in Nineveh.

That day whereof we keep record,
When near thy city-gates the Lord
Sheltered His Jonah with a gourd,
This sun (I said), here present, pour'd
Even thus this shadow that I see.
This shadow has been shed the same
From sun and moon,—from lamps which came
For prayer,—from fifteen days of flame,
The last while smouldered to a name
Sardanapalus' Nineveh.

Within thy shadow, haply, once
Sennacherib has knelt, whose sons
Smote him between the altar-stones:
Or pale Semiramis her zones
Of gold, her incense brought to thee,
In love for grace, in war for aid: . . .
Ay, and who else? . . . till 'neath thy shade
Within his trenches newly made
Last year the Christian knelt and pray'd—
Not to thy strength—in Nineveh.

Now, thou poor god, within this hall
Where the blank windows blind the wall
From pedestal to pedestal,
The kind of light shall on thee fall
Which London takes the day to be:
While school-foundations in the act
Of holiday, three files compact,
Shall learn to view thee as a fact
Connected with that zealous tract:
"Rome,—Babylon and Nineveh."

Deemed they of this, those worshippers,
When, in some mythic chain of verse
Which man shall not again rehearse,
The faces of thy ministers
Yearned pale with bitter ecstasy?
Greece, Egypt, Rome,—did any god
Before whose feet men knelt unshod
Deem that in this unblest abode
Another scarce more unknown god
Should house with him from Nineveh?

Ah! in what quarries lay the stone
From which this pillared pile has grown,
Unto man's need how long unknown,
Since those thy temples, court and cone,
Rose far in desert history?
Ah! what is here that does not lie
All strange to thine awakened eye?
Ah! what is here can testify
(Save that dumb presence of the sky)
Unto thy day and Nineveh?

Why, of those mummies in the room
Above, there might indeed have come
One out of Egypt to thy home,
An alien. Nay, but were not some
Of these thine own "antiquity"?
And now,—they and their gods and thou
All relics here together,—now
Whose profit? whether bull or cow,
Isis or Ibis, who or how,
Whether of Thebes or Nineveh?

The consecrated metals found,
And ivory tablets, underground,
Winged teraphim and creatures crown'd,
When air and daylight filled the mound,
Fell into dust immediately.
And even as these, the images
Of awe and worship,—even as these,—
So, smitten with the sun's increase,
Her glory mouldered and did cease
From immemorial Nineveh.

The day her builders made their halt,
Those cities of the lake of salt
Stood firmly 'stablished without fault,
Made proud with pillars of basalt,
With sardonyx and porphyry.
The day that Jonah bore abroad
To Nineveh the voice of God,
A brackish lake lay in his road,
Where erst Pride fixed her sure abode,
As then in Royal Nineveh.

The day when he, Pride's lord and Man's,
Showed all the kingdoms at a glance
To Him before whose countenance
The years recede, the years advance,
And said, Fall down and worship me :—
'Mid all the pomp beneath that look,
Then stirred there, haply, some rebuke,
Where to the wind the Salt Pools shook,
And in those tracts, of life forsook,
That knew thee not, O Nineveh !

Delicate harlot !   On thy throne
Thou with a world beneath thee prone
In state for ages sat'st alone ;
And needs were years and lustres flown
Ere strength of man could vanquish thee :
Whom even thy victor foes must bring,
Still royal, among maids that sing
As with doves' voices, taboring
Upon their breasts, unto the King,—
A kingly conquest, Nineveh !

A LONDON GARLAND

. . . Here woke my thought. The wind's slow sway
Had waxed ; and like the human play
Of scorn that smiling spreads away,
The sunshine shivered off the day :
The callous wind, it seemed to me,
Swept up the shadow from the ground :
And pale as whom the Fates astound,
The god forlorn stood winged and crown'd :
Within I knew the cry lay bound
Of the dumb soul of Nineveh.

And as I turned, my sense half shut
Still saw the crowds of kerb and rut
Go past as marshalled to the strut
Of ranks in gypsum quaintly cut.
It seemed in one same pageantry
They followed forms which had been erst ;
To pass, till on my sight should burst
That future of the best or worst
When some may question which was first,
Of London or of Nineveh.

For as that Bull-god once did stand
And watched the burial-clouds of sand,
Till these at last without a hand
Rose o'er his eyes, another land,
And blinded him with Destiny :—
So may he stand again ; till now,
In ships of unknown sail and prow,
Some tribe of the Australian plough
Bear him afar,—a relic now
Of London, not of Nineveh !

Or it may chance indeed that when
Man's age is hoary among men,—
His centuries threescore and ten,—
His furthest childhood shall seem then
More clear than later times may be :
Who, finding in this desert place
This form, shall hold us for some race
That walked not in Christ's lowly ways,
But bowed its pride and vowed its praise
Unto the God of Nineveh.

The smile rose first,—anon drew nigh
The thought : . . . Those heavy wings spread high,
So sure of flight, which do not fly ;
That set gaze never on the sky ;
Those scriptured flanks it cannot see ;
Its crown, a brow-contracting load ;
Its planted feet which trust the sod : . . .
(So grew the image as I trod :)—
O Nineveh, was this thy God,—
Thine also, mighty Nineveh?

DANTE GABRIEL ROSSETTI
(1828-1882).

ST. JAMES'S STREET

ST. JAMES'S STREET, of classic fame,
    For Fashion still is seen there:
St. James's Street? I know the name,
    I almost think I've been there!
Why, that's where *Sacharissa* sigh'd
    When Waller read his ditty;
Where Byron lived, and Gibbon died,
    And Alvanley was witty.

A famous Street! To yonder Park
    Young Churchill stole in class-time;
Come, gaze on fifty men of mark,
    And then recall the past time.
The *plats* at White's, the play at *Crock's*,
    The bumpers to Miss Gunning;
The *bonhomie* of Charley Fox,
    And Selwyn's ghastly funning.

The dear old Street of clubs and *cribs*,
    As north and south it stretches,
Still seems to smack of Rolliad squibs,
    And Gillray's fiercer sketches;
The quaint old dress, the grand old style,
    The *mots*, the racy stories;
The wine, the dice, the wit, the bile—
    The hate of Whigs and Tories.

At dusk, when I am strolling there,
    Dim forms will rise around me,
Lepel flits past me in her chair,—
    And Congreve's airs astound me!

A LONDON GARLAND

And once Nell Gwynne, a frail young Sprite,
    Look'd kindly when I met her;
I shook my head, perhaps,—but quite
    Forgot to quite forget her.

The Street is still a lively tomb
    For rich, and gay, and clever;
The crops of dandies bud and bloom,
    And die as fast as ever.
Now gilded youth loves cutty pipes,
    And slang that's rather *scaring;*
It can't approach its prototypes
    In taste, or tone, or bearing.

In Brummel's day of buckle shoes,
    Lawn cravats, and roll collars,
They'd fight, and woo, and bet—and lose
    Like gentlemen and scholars:
I'm glad young men should go the pace,
    I half forgive *Old Rapid;*
These louts disgrace their name and race—
    So vicious and so vapid!

Worse times may come. *Bon ton*, indeed,
    Will then be quite forgotten,
And all we much revere will speed
    From ripe to worse than rotten:
Let grass then sprout between yon stones,
    And owls then roost at Boodle's,
For Echo will hurl back the tones
    Of screaming *Yankee Doodles.*

I love the haunts of old Cockaigne,
    Where wit and wealth were squander'd;
The halls that tell of hoop and train,
    Where grace and rank have wander'd;
Those halls where ladies fair and leal
    First ventured to adore me!
Something of that old love I feel
    For this old Street before me.

1867.
                                         Frederick Locker-Lampson
                                                (1821-1895).

PICCADILLY

*Her eyes and her hair
        Are superb;
She stands in despair
        On the kerb.
Quick, stranger, advance
        To her aid:
She's across, with a glance
        You're repaid.
She's fair, and you're tall,
        Fal-la-la!—
What will come of it all?
        Chi lo sa!*
        CUPID ON THE CROSSING.

ICCADILLY! Shops, palaces, bustle, and breeze,
The whirring of wheels and the murmur of trees;
By night or by day, whether noisy or stilly,
Whatever my mood is, I love Piccadilly.

A LONDON GARLAND

Wet nights, when the gas on the pavement is streaming,
And young Love is watching, and old Love is dreaming,
And beauty is whirling to conquest, where shrilly
Cremona makes nimble thy toes, Piccadilly!

Bright days when a stroll is my afternoon wont,
And I meet all the people I do know, or don't,
Here is jolly old Brown, and his fair daughter Lillie—
No wonder, young Pilgrim, you like Piccadilly!

See yonder pair riding, how fondly they saunter,
She smiles on her Poet, whose heart's in a canter!
Some envy her spouse, and some covet her filly,
He envies them both,—he's an ass, Piccadilly!

Now were I such a bride, with a slave at my feet,
I would choose me a house in my favourite street;
Yes or no—I would carry my point, willy-nilly:
If "no,"—pick a quarrel; if "yes,"—Piccadilly!

From Primrose balcony, long ages ago,
"Old Q." sat at gaze,—who now passes below?
A frolicsome statesman, the Man of the Day;
A laughing philosopher, gallant and gay;

Never darling of fortune more manfully trod,
Full of years, full of fame, and the world at his nod,
Can the thought reach his heart, and then leave it more chilly—
Old P. or old Q.,—"I must quit Piccadilly"?

Life is chequer'd; a patchwork of smiles and of frowns;
We value its ups, let us muse on its downs;
There's a side that is bright; it will then turn us t'other;
One turn, if a good one, deserves yet another.
These downs are delightful, these ups are not hilly,—
Let us try one more turn ere we quit Piccadilly.

FREDERICK LOCKER-LAMPSON.

SUNDAY AT HAMPSTEAD

(An Idle Idyll by a very humble member of the great and noble London mob)

I

THIS is the Heath of Hampstead,
There is the dome of Saint Paul's;
Beneath, on the serried house-tops,
A chequered lustre falls:

And the mighty city of London,
Under the clouds and the light,
Seems a low wet beach, half shingle,
With a few sharp rocks upright.

Here will we sit, my darling,
And dream an hour away:
The donkeys are hurried and worried,
But we are not donkeys to-day:

Through all the weary week, dear,
We toil in the murk down there,
Tied to a desk and a counter,
A patient stupid pair!

But on Sunday we slip our tether,
And away from the smoke and the smirch;
Too grateful to God for His Sabbath
To shut its hours in a church.

Away to the green, green country,
Under the open sky;
Where the earth's sweet breath is incense
And the lark sings psalms on high.

On Sunday we're Lord and Lady,
With ten times the love and glee
Of those pale and languid rich ones
Who are always and never free.

They drawl and stare and simper,
So fine and cold and staid,
Like exquisite waxwork figures
That must be kept in the shade!

We can laugh out loud when merry,
We can romp at kiss-in-the-ring,
We can take our beer at a public,
We can loll on the grass and sing. . . .

Would you grieve very much, my darling,
If all yon low wet shore
Were drowned by a mighty flood tide,
And we never toiled there more?

Wicked?—there is no sin, dear,
In an idle dreamer's head;
He turns the world topsy-turvy
To prove that his soul's not dead.

I am sinking, sinking, sinking;
It is hard to sit upright!
Your lap is the softest pillow!
Good night, my Love, good night!

.

III

Was it hundreds of years ago, my Love,
  Was it thousands of miles away,
That two poor creatures we know, my Love,
  Were toiling day by day;
      Were toiling weary, weary,
      With many myriads more,
      In a City dark and dreary
      On a sullen river's shore?

A LONDON GARLAND

Was it truly a fact or a dream, my Love?
  I think my brain still reels,
And my ears still throbbing seem, my Love,
  With the rush and the clang of wheels;
      Of a vast machinery roaring
      For ever in skyless gloom,
      Where the poor slaves peace imploring,
      Found peace alone in the tomb.

Was it hundreds of years ago, my Love,
  Was it thousands of miles away?
Or was it a dream to show, my Love,
  The rapture of to-day?
      This day of holy splendour,
      This Sabbath of rich rest
      Wherein to God we render
      All praise by being blest.

                      JAMES THOMSON
                      (1834-1882).

A LONDON PLANE-TREE

REEN is the plane-tree in the square,
    The other trees are brown;
They droop and pine for country air;
    The plane-tree loves the town.

Here, from my garret-pane, I mark
    The plane-tree bud and blow,
Shed her recuperative bark,
    And spread her shade below.

Among her branches in and out,
    The city breezes play;
The dun fog wraps her round about;
    Above, the smoke curls gray.

Others the country take for choice,
    And hold the town in scorn;
But she has listened to the voice
    On city breezes borne.

                  AMY LEVY
                  (1862-1889).

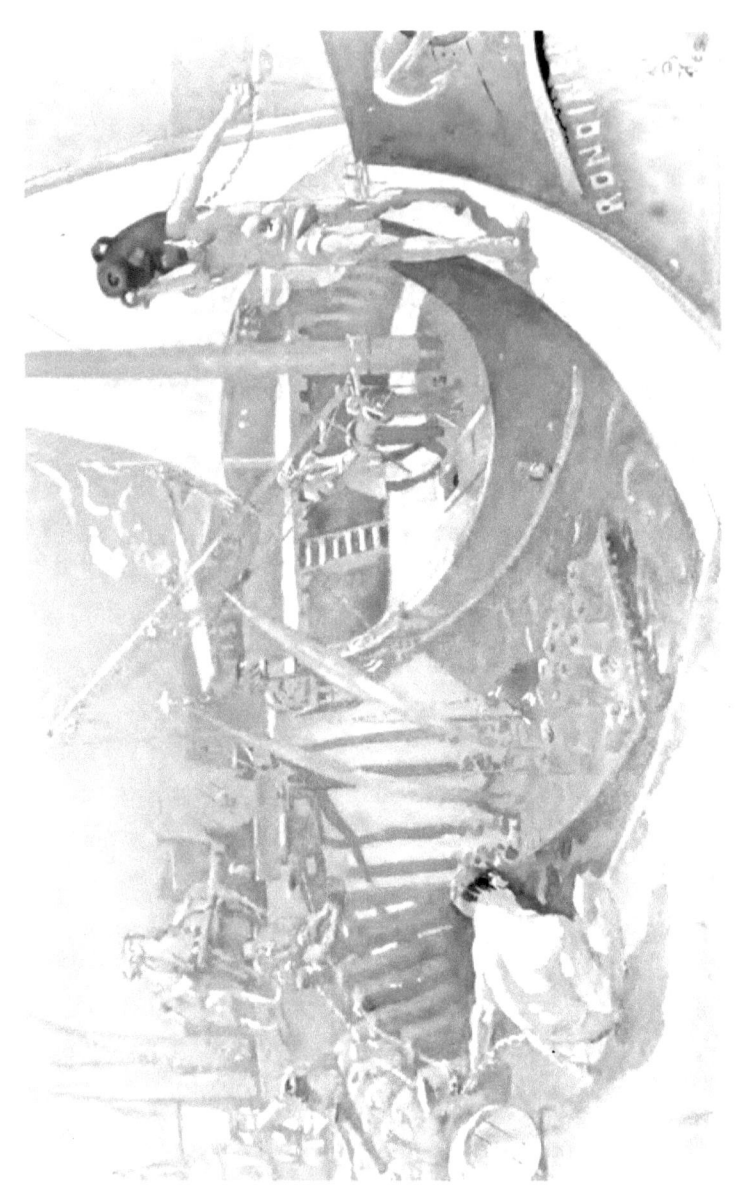

A DREAM

ORGET six counties overhung with smoke,
    Forget the snorting steam and piston stroke,
    Forget the spreading of the hideous town;
    Think rather of the pack-horse on the down,
    And dream of London, small, and white, and cle
The clear Thames bordered by its gardens green;
Think, that below bridge the green lapping waves
Smite some few keels that bear Levantine staves,
Cut from the yew wood on the burnt-up hill,
And pointed jars that Greek hands toiled to fill,
And treasured scanty spice from some far sea,
Florence gold-cloth, and Ypres napery,
And cloth of Bruges, and hogsheads of Guienne;
While nigh the throng'd wharf Geoffrey Chaucer's pen
Moves over bills of lading. . . .

                              WILLIAM MORRIS.

LONDON SNOW

HEN men were all asleep the snow came flying,
    In large white flakes falling on the city brown,
    Stealthily and perpetually settling and loosely lying,
        Hushing the latest traffic of the drowsy town ;
        Deadening, muffling, stifling its murmurs failing ;
Lazily and incessantly floating down and down :
    Silently sifting and veiling road, roof and railing ;
Hiding difference, making unevenness even,
Into angles and crevices softly drifting and sailing.
    All night it fell, and when full inches seven
It lay in the depth of its uncompacted lightness,
Its clouds blew off from a high and frosty heaven ;
    And all awoke earlier for the unaccustomed brightness
Of the winter dawning, the strange unheavenly glare :
The eye marvelled—marvelled at the dazzling whiteness ;
    The ear hearkened to the stillness of the solemn air ;
No sound of wheel rumbling nor of foot falling,
And the busy morning cries came thin and spare.
    Then boys I heard, as they went to school, calling,
They gathered up the crystal manna to freeze
Their tongues with tasting, their hands with snow-balling ;
    Or rioted in a drift, plunging up to the knees ;
Or peering up from under the white-mossed wonder,
" O look at the trees ! " they cried, " O look at the trees ! "
    With lessened load a few carts creak and blunder,
Following along the white deserted way,
A country company long dispersed asunder :
    When now already the sun, in pale display
Standing by Paul's high dome, spread forth below
His sparkling beams, and awoke the stir of the day.
    For now doors open, and war is waged with the snow ;
And trains of sombre men, past tale of number,

A LONDON GARLAND

Tread long brown paths, as toward their toil they go :
    But even for them awhile no cares encumber
Their minds diverted ; the daily word unspoken,
The daily thoughts of labour and sorrow slumber
At the sight of the beauty that greets them, for the charm they
      broken.

ROBERT BRIDGES.

A THAMES SUBURB

E left the city when the summer day
    Had verged already on its hot decline,
And charmèd Indolence in languor lay
    In her gay gardens, 'neath her towers divine:
      "Farewell," we said, "dear city of youth and dream!"
And in our boat we stepped and took the stream.

All through that idle afternoon we strayed
    Upon our proposed travel well begun,
As loitering by the woodland's dreamy shade,
    Past shallow islets floating in the sun,
      Or searching down the banks for rarer flowers
We lingered out the pleasurable hours.

Till when that loveliest came, which mowers home
    Turns from their longest labour, as we steered
Along a straitened channel flecked with foam,
    We lost our landscape wide, and slowly neared
      An ancient bridge, that like a blind wall lay
Low on its buried vaults to block the way.

Then soon the narrow tunnels broader showed,
    Where with its arches three it sucked the mass
Of water, that in swirl thereunder flowed,
    Or stood piled at the piers waiting to pass;
      And pulling for the middle span, we drew
The tender blades aboard and floated through.

But past the bridge what change we found below!
The stream, that all day long had laughed and played

Betwixt the happy shires, ran dark and slow,
And with its easy flood no murmur made :
And weeds spread on its surface, and about
The stagnant margin reared their stout heads out.

Upon the left high elms, with giant wood
Skirting the water-meadows, interwove
Their slumbrous crowns, o'ershadowing where they stood
The floor and heavy pillars of the grove :
And in the shade, through reeds and sedges dank,
A footpath led along the moated bank.

Across, all down the right, an old brick wall,
Above and o'er the channel, red did lean ;
Here buttressed up, and bulging there to fall,
Tufted with grass and plants and lichen green ;
And crumbling to the flood, which at its base
Slid gently nor disturbed its mirrored face.

Sheer on the wall the houses rose, their backs
All windowless, neglected and awry,
With tottering coins, and crooked chimney stacks ;
And here and there an unused door, set high
Above the fragments of its mouldering stair,
With rail and broken step led out on air.

Beyond, deserted wharfs and vacant sheds,
With empty boats and barges moored along,
And rafts half sunken, fringed with weedy shreds,
And sodden beams, once soaked to season strong.
No sight of man, nor sight of life, no stroke,
No voice the somnolence and silence broke.

Then I who rowed leant on my oar, whose drip
Fell without sparkle, and I rowed no more ;
And he that steered moved neither hand nor lip,
But turned his wondering eye from shore to shore ;
And our trim boat let her swift motion die,
Between the dim reflections floating by.

ROBERT BRIDGES.

AN AUTUMN IDYLL

"Sweet Themmes! runne softly, till I end my song."—SPENSER

LAWRENCE   FRANK   JACK

LAWRENCE

HERE, where the beech-nuts drop among the grasses,
    Push the boat in, and throw the rope ashore.
Jack, hand me out the claret and the glasses;
    Here let us sit. We landed here before.

FRANK

Jack's undecided. Say, *formose puer*,
    Bent in a dream above the "water wan,"
Shall we row higher, for the reeds are fewer,
    There by the pollards, where you see the swan?

JACK

Hist! That's a pike. Look—nose against the river
    Gaunt as a wolf,—the sly old privateer!
Enter a gudgeon. Snap,—a gulp, a shiver;—
    Exit the gudgeon. Let us anchor here.

FRANK (*in the grass*)

Jove, what a day! Black Care upon the crupper
    Nods at his post, and slumbers in the sun;
Half of Theocritus, with a touch of Tupper,
    Churns in my head. The frenzy has begun!

LAWRENCE

Sing to us then. Damoetas in a choker,
    Much out of tune, will edify the rooks.

FRANK

Sing you again. So musical a croaker
    Surely will draw the fish upon the hooks.

JACK

Sing while you may. The beard of manhood still is
    Faint on your cheeks, but I, alas! am old.
Doubtless you yet believe in Amaryllis;—
    Sing me of Her, whose name may not be told.

FRANK

Listen, O Thames! His budding beard is riper,
    Say, by a week. Well, Lawrence, shall we sing?

LAWRENCE

Yes, if you will. But ere I play the piper,
    Let him declare the prize he has to bring.

JACK

Hear then, my Shepherds. Lo, to him accounted
    First in the song, a Pipe I will impart;—
This, my Belovéd, marvellously mounted,
    Amber and foam,—a miracle of art.

LAWRENCE

Lordly the gift. O Muse of many numbers,
    Grant me a soft alliterative song!

FRANK

Me too, O Muse! And when the Umpire slumbers,
    Sting him with gnats a summer evening long.

LAWRENCE

Not in a cot, begarlanded of spiders,
    Not where the brook traditionally "purls,"—
No, in the Row, supreme among the riders,
    Seek I the gem,—the paragon of girls.

A LONDON GARLAND

FRANK

Not in the waste of column and of coping,
    Not in the sham and stucco of a square,—
No, on a June-lawn, to the water sloping,
    Stands she I honour, beautifully fair.

LAWRENCE

Dark-haired is mine, with splendid tresses plaited
    Back from the brows, imperially curled;
Calm as a grand, far-looking Caryatid,
    Holding the roof that covers in a world.

FRANK

Dark-haired is mine, with breezy ripples swinging
    Loose as a vine-branch blowing in the morn;
Eyes like the morning, mouth for ever singing,
    Blithe as a bird new risen from the corn.

LAWRENCE

Best is the song with music interwoven;
    Mine's a musician,—musical at heart,—
Throbs to the gathered grieving of Beethoven,
    Sways to the light coquetting of Mozart.

FRANK

Best? You should hear mine trilling out a ballad,
    Queen at a pic-nic, leader of the glees,
Not too divine to toss you up a salad,
    Great in Sir Roger danced among the trees.

LAWRENCE

Ah, when the thick night flares with drooping torches,
    Ah, when the crush-room empties of the swarm,
Pleasant the hand that, in the gusty porches,
    Light as a snow-flake, settles on your arm.

FRANK

Better the twilight and the cheery chatting,—
    Better the dim, forgotten garden-seat,
Where one may lie, and watch the fingers tatting,
    Lounging with Bran or Bevis at her feet.

LAWRENCE

All worship mine. Her purity doth hedge her
    Round with so delicate divinity, that men,
Stained to the soul with money-bag and ledger,
    Bend to the goddess, manifest again.

FRANK

None worship mine. But some, I fancy, love her,—
    Cynics to boot. I know the children run,
Seeing her come, for naught that I discover,
    Save that she brings the summer and the sun.

LAWRENCE

Mine is a Lady, beautiful and queenly,
    Crowned with a sweet, continual control,
Grandly forbearing, lifting life serenely
    E'en to her own nobility of soul.

FRANK

Mine is a Woman, kindly beyond measure,
    Fearless in praising, faltering in blame;
Simply devoted to other people's pleasure,—
    Jack's sister Florence,—now you know her name.

LAWRENCE

"Jack's sister Florence!" Never, Francis, never.
    Jack, do you hear? Why, it was she I meant.
She like the country! Ah, she's far too clever.

FRANK

    There you are wrong. I knew her down in Kent.

LAWRENCE

You'll get a sunstroke, standing with your head bare.
    Sorry to differ. Jack—the word's with you.

FRANK

How is it, Umpire? Though the motto's threadbare,
    "*Cœlum, non animum,*" is, I take it, true.

Jack

"*Souvent femme varie*," as a rule is truer;
    Flattered, I'm sure,—but both of you romance.
Happy to further suit of either wooer,
    Merely observing—you haven't got a chance.

Lawrence

Yes. But the Pipe—

Frank

    The Pipe is what we care for,—

Jack

    Well, in this case, I scarcely need explain,
Judgment of mine were indiscreet, and therefore,—
    Peace to you both. The Pipe I shall retain.

Austin Dobson.

THE MALTWORM'S MADRIGAL

DRINK of the Ale of Southwark, I drink of the Ale of Che
At noon I dream on the settle; at night I cannot sleep;
For my love, my love it groweth; I waste me all the day;
And when I see sweet Alison, I know not what to say.

The sparrow when he spieth his Dear upon the tree,
He beateth to his little wing; he chirketh lustily;
But when I see sweet Alison, the words begin to fail;
I wot that I shall die of Love—an I die not of Ale.

Her lips are like the muscadel; her brows are black as ink;
Her eyes are bright as beryl stones that in the tankard wink;
But when she sees me coming, she shrilleth out—"Tee-Hee!
Fye on thy ruddy nose, Cousin, what lackest thou of me?"

"Fye on thy ruddy nose, Cousin! Why be thine eyes so small?
Why go thy legs tap-lappetty like men that fear to fall?
Why is thy leathern doublet besmeared with stain and spot?
Go to. Thou art no man (she saith), thou art a Pottlepot!"

"No man," i' faith. "No man!" she saith. And "Pottlepot" there
"Thou sleepest like our dog all day; thou drink'st as fishes do."
I would that I were Tibb the dog; he wags at her his tail;
Or would that I were fish, perdy, and all the sea were Ale!

So I drink of the Ale of Southwark, I drink of the Ale of Chepe;
All day I dream in the sunlight; I dream and eke I weep.
But little lore of loving can any flagon teach,
For when my tongue is loosèd most, then most I lose my speech.

AUSTIN DOBSO

TOMMY

I WENT into a public-'ouse to get a pint o' beer,
  The publican 'e up an' sez, "We serve no red-coats here."
  The girls be'ind the bar they laughed an' giggled fit to die,
  I outs into the street again an' to myself sez I:
    O it's Tommy this, an' Tommy that, an' "Tommy, go away";
  But it's "Thank you, Mister Atkins," when the band begins to play;
  The band begins to play, my boys, the band begins to play,
    O it's "Thank you, Mister Atkins," when the band begins to play.

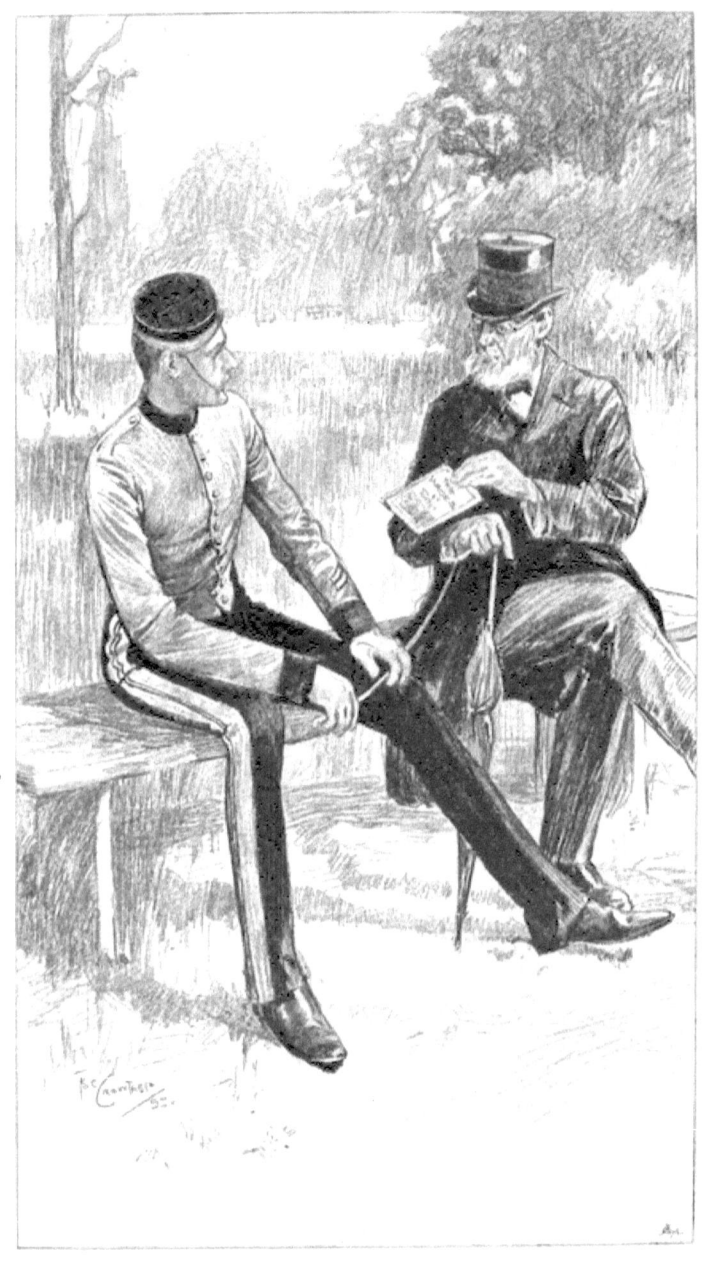

nt into a theatre as sober as could be,
gave a drunk civilian room, but 'adn't none for me ;
sent me to the gallery or round the music-'alls,
when it comes to fightin', Lord! they'll shove me in the stalls!
    For it's Tommy this, an' Tommy that, an' "Tommy, wait
        outside ";
    But it's "Special train for Atkins" when the trooper's on the tide,
    The troopship's on the tide, my boys, the troopship's on the tide,
    O it's "Special train for Atkins" when the trooper's on the tide.

makin' mock o' uniforms that guard you while you sleep
eaper than them uniforms, an' they're starvation cheap ;
ustlin' drunken soldiers when they're goin' large a bit
e times better business than paradin' in full kit.
    Then it's Tommy this, an' Tommy that, an' "Tommy, 'ow's
        yer soul?"
    But it's "Thin red line of 'eroes" when the drums begin to roll,
    The drums begin to roll, my boys, the drums begin to roll,
    O it's "Thin red line of 'eroes" when the drums begin to roll.

iren't no thin red 'eroes, nor we aren't no blackguards too,
ingle men in barricks, most remarkable like you ;
f sometimes our conduck isn't all your fancy paints,
, single men in barricks don't grow into plaster saints ;
    While it's Tommy this, an' Tommy that, an' "Tommy, fall be'ind,"
    But it's "Please to walk in front, sir," when there's trouble in the
        wind,
    There's trouble in the wind, my boys, there's trouble in the wind,
    O it's "Please to walk in front, sir," when there's trouble in the
        wind.

talk o' better food for us, an' schools, an' fires, an' all :
l wait for extry rations if you treat us rational.
t mess about the cook-room slops, but prove it to our face
Widow's Uniform is not the soldier-man's disgrace.
    For it's Tommy this, an' Tommy that, an' "Chuck him out, the
        brute!"
    But it's "Saviour of 'is country" when the guns begin to shoot ;
    An' it's Tommy this, an' Tommy that, an' anything you please ;
    An' Tommy ain't a bloomin' fool—you bet that Tommy sees!

RUDYARD KIPLING.

UNDER THE SPEAKER'S GALLERY

N all the comedy of human things
What is more mirthful than for those, who sit
Far from the great world's vain imaginings,
To mingle in its war of words and wit,
A listener here, when Greek meets Greek, Fox
At question time in the Queen's Parliament?
'Tis the arena of old Rome.   Here meet
More than mere Dacians on mere slaughter bent.
Yonder and close to Mr. Speaker's chair,
Enfolding all things in a net of words,
Stands our first gymnast.   Let the rest beware.
The Tory Stafford, with voice sweet as bird's,
Shall answer him anon, or bolder borne
And if luck favours, from the nether herds
A voice of patriot wrath shall rise in scorn,
Or even young Cassius blow his windy horn.

WILFRID SCAWEN BLUNT.

THE LONDON SEASON

I STILL love London in the month of May,
By an old habit, spite of dust and din.
I love the fair adulterous world, whose way
Is by the pleasant banks of Serpentine.
I love the worshippers at fashion's shrine,
The flowers, the incense, and the pageantry
Of generations which still ask a sign
Of that dear god, whose votary am I.
I love the "greetings in the market-place,"
The jargon of the clubs. I love to view
The "gilded youth" who at the window pass,
For ever smiling smiles for ever new.
I love these men and women at their task
Of hunting pleasure. Hope, mysterious too,
Touches my arm and points, and seems to ask,
"And you, have you no Juliet in the masque?"

WILFRID SCAWEN BLUNT.

GOODWOOD

TO the high breezes of the Goodwood Down
   London has fled, and there awhile forgets
   Its weariness of limb on lawns new-mown
   And in green shadows all its wars and frets.
   Thither we too will bring our calumets
In sign of peace restored o'er fashion slain,
Weaning our souls from folly with small bets
Of gloves and crowns with laughing ringwomen.
The sport is fair, luck fair, and Nature's face
Fairest of all. We neither make nor mar
A fortune here. Yet we were rich with less
Than this week's pleasure conquered from the year.
I would not for a million not have seen
Fred Archer finish upon Guinevere.
Hark! They are off again, a half mile spin,
Four of the dozen backed and bound to win.

WILFRID SCAWEN BLUNT.

A DAY AT HAMPTON COURT

IT is our custom, once in every year,
    Mine and two others', when the chestnut trees
    Are white at Bushey, Ascot being near,
    To drive to Hampton Court, and there, at ease
    In that most fair of English palaces,
Spend a long summer's day. What better cheer
Than the old "Greyhound's," seek it where you please?
And where a royal garden statelier?
The morning goes in tennis, a four set,
With George the marker. 'Tis a game for Gods,
Full of return and volley at the net,
And laughter and mirth-making episodes
Not wholly classic. But the afternoon
Finds us punt-fishing idly with our rods,
Nodding and half in dreams, till all too soon
Darkness and dinner drive us back to town.

                      WILFRID SCAWEN BLUNT.

IN AN OLD CITY CHURCH

ONE dull, foggy day in December,
When biting and bleak was the air,
I once lost my way, I remember,
And paused in a quaint City square.
Though lacking all splendour or gladness
The flavour of good long ago
Clung close to the place in its sadness,
And grave-yard half covered with snow ;
While the black, puny branches, all leafless and bare,
Seemed to add to the gloom of this dull City square

The railings were rusty and rimy,
The church looked so mouldy and grim ;
The houses seemed haunted and grimy,
The windows were gruesome and dim.
The iron gate scrooped on its hinges,
The clock struck a querulous chime,
As though it were feeling some twinges
'Twas almost forgotten by Time.
But I opened the door, and the picture was fair,
In the fine ancient church, in this sad City square !

A fair little lass, holly-laden—
With eyes of cerulean blue—
Is helping a sweet dark-eyed maiden
Twine ivy with laurel and yew ;
How busy the deft taper fingers !
What taste and what art they display !
How lovingly each of them lingers,
Adjusting a leaf or a spray !—
I close the door softly, I've no business there,
And drift out in the fog of the grim City square.

IN THE RAIN

AIN in the glimmering street—
Murmurous, rhythmical beat;
Shadows that flicker and fly;
Blue of wet road, of wet sky,
(Gray in the depths and the heights);
Orange of numberless lights,
Shapes fleeting on, going by.

Figures, fantastical, grim—
Figures, prosaical, tame,
Each with chameleon-stain,
Dun in the crepuscle dim,
Red in the nimbus of flame—
Glance through the veil of the rain.

Rain in the measureless street,
Vistas of orange and blue;
Music of echoing feet,
Pausing and pacing anew.

Rain and the clamour of wheels,
Splendour, and shadow, and sound;
Coloured confusion that reels
Lost in the twilight around.

When I lie hid from the light,
Stark, with the turf overhead,
Still, on a rainy Spring night,
I shall come back from the dead.

A LONDON GARLAND

Turn then and look for me here
Stealing the shadows along;
Look for me—I shall be near,
Deep in the heart of the throng:

Here, where the current runs rife,
Careless, and doleful, and gay,
Moving, and motley, and strong,
Good in its sport, in its strife.

Ah, might I be—might I stay—
Only for ever and aye,
Living and looking on life!

ROSAMOND MARRIOTT-WATSON.

A RIDDLE OF THE THAMES

T windows that from Westminster
Look southward to the Lollard's Tower,
She sat, my lovely friend. A blur
Of gilded mist,—('twas morn's first hour),—
Made vague the world : and in the gleam
Shivered the half-awakened stream.

Through tinted vapour looming large,
Ambiguous shapes obscurely rode.
She gazed where many a laden barge
Like some dim-moving saurian showed.
And 'midst them, lo! two swans appeared,
And proudly up the river steered.

A LONDON GARLAND

Two stately swans! What did they there?
Whence came they? Whither would they go?
Think of them,—things so faultless fair,—
'Mid the black shipping down below!
On through the rose and gold they passed,
And melted in the morn at last.

Ah, can it be, that they had come
Where Thames in sullied glory flows,
Fugitive rebels, tired of some
Secluded lake's ornate repose,
Eager to taste the life that pours
Its muddier wave 'twixt mightier shores?

We ne'er shall know : our wonderment
No barren certitude shall mar.
They left behind them, as they went,
A dream than knowledge ampler far ;
And from our world they sailed away
Into some visionary day.

WILLIAM WATSON

IN FOUNTAIN COURT

THE fountain murmuring of sleep,
    A drowsy tune;
The flickering green of leaves that keep
    The light of June;
    Peace, through a slumbering afternoon,
The peace of June.

A waiting ghost, in the blue sky
    The white curved moon;
June, hushed and breathless, waits, and I
    Wait too, with June;
Come, through the lingering afternoon
    Soon, love, come soon.

ARTHUR SYMONS.

A LOAFER

 HANG about the streets all day,
At night I hang about;
I sleep a little when I may,
But rise betimes the morning's scout;
For through the year I always hear
Afar, aloft, a ghostly shout.

My clothes are worn to threads and loops;
My skin shows here and there;
About my face like seaweed droops
My tangled beard, my tangled hair;
From cavernous and shaggy brows
My stony eyes untroubled stare.

I move from eastern wretchedness
Through Fleet Street and the Strand;
And as the pleasant people press
I touch them softly with my hand,
Perhaps to know that still I go
Alive about a living land.

For, far in front the clouds are riven;
I hear the ghostly cry,
As if a still voice fell from heaven
To where sea-whelmed the drowned folk lie
In sepulchres no tempest stirs
And only eyeless things pass by.

A LONDON GARLAND

In Piccadilly spirits pass:
Oh, eyes and cheeks that glow!
Oh, strength and comeliness! Alas,
The lustrous health is earth I know
From shrinking eyes that recognise
No brother in my rags and woe.

I know no handicraft, no art,
But I have conquered fate;
For I have chosen the better part,
And neither hope, nor fear, nor hate.
With placid breath on pain and death,
My certain alms, alone I wait.

And daily, nightly comes the call,
The pale unechoing note,
The faint "Aha!" sent from the wall
Of heaven, but from no ruddy throat
Of human breed or seraph's seed,
A phantom voice that cries by rote.

JOHN DAVIDSON.

BALLADE OF CLEOPATRA'S NEEDLE

E giant shades of Ra and Tum,
Ye ghosts of gods Egyptian,
If murmurs of our planet come
To exiles in the precincts wan
Where, fetish or Olympian,
To help or harm no more ye list,
Look down, if look ye may, and scan
This monument in London mist!

Behold, the hieroglyphs are dumb
That once were read of him that ran
When seistron, cymbal, trump, and drum
Wild music of the Bull began;
When through the chanting priestly clan
Walk'd Ramses, and the high sun kiss'd
This stone, with blessing scored and ban—
This monument in London mist.

The stone endures though gods be numb;
Though human effort, plot, and plan
Be sifted, drifted, like the sum
Of sands in wastes Arabian.

What king may deem him more than man,
What priest says Faith can Time resist
While *this* endures to mark their span—
This monument in London mist?

Envoy

Prince, the stone's shade on your divan
Falls ; it is longer than ye wist :
It preaches, as Time's gnomon can,
This monument in London mist !

Andrew

BALLADE OF SUMMER

HEN strawberry pottles are common and cheap,
   Ere elms be black, or limes be sere,
   When midnight dances are murdering sleep,
   Then comes in the sweet o' the year!
   And far from Fleet Street, far from here,
The Summer is Queen in the length of the land,
And moonlit nights they are soft and clear,
When fans for a penny are sold in the Strand!

When clamour that doves in the lindens keep
Mingles with musical plash of the weir,
Where drowned green tresses of crowsfoot creep,
Then comes in the sweet o' the year!
And better a crust and a beaker of beer,
With rose-hung hedges on either hand,
Than a palace in town and a prince's cheer,
When fans for a penny are sold in the Strand!

When big trout late in the twilight leap,
When cuckoo clamoureth far and near,
When glittering scythes in the hayfield reap,
Then comes in the sweet o' the year!
And it's oh to sail, with the wind to steer,
Where kine knee-deep in the water stand,
On a Highland loch, on a Lowland mere,
When fans for a penny are sold in the Strand!

Envoy

Friend, with the fops while we dawdle here,
Then comes in the sweet o' the year!
And the Summer runs out, like grains of sand,
When fans for a penny are sold in the Strand!

ANDREW l

AT A DISTANCE

EAR, you are farther off from me
    Than my gaunt garret from the sky,
Or parching desert from the sea,
    Or sound and laughter from a sigh.

I know you breathe our civic air,
    And sometimes down some dreary street
I see you pass divinely fair,
    And look for roses at your feet.

And sometimes through St. James's trees
    You drive, a goddess of the light;
And I can see you, when I please,
    Behind the level lamps at night:

Where from some corner I can stare
    Across that line of yellow fire,
And feed upon your face and hair—
    The pain of exquisite desire.

What does it matter? ·Who will care,
    Another hundred years or so,
That I wrote verses to your hair,
    Whose tresses then in grass may grow?

                    JUSTIN HUNTLY M'C.

And I can see You when I please Behind the level Lamps at Night.

THE LITTLE DANCERS

(By permission from the Pall Mall Gazette)

ONELY, save for a few faint stars, the sky
   Dreams ; and lonely below the little street
   Into its gloom retires, secluded and shy.
   Scarcely the dumb roar enters this soft retreat ;
   And all is dark ; save where come flooding the rays
From a tavern window : there, to the brisk measure
Of an organ that down in an alley merrily plays,
Two children, all alone and no one by,
Holding their tattered frocks, through an airy maze
Of motion lightly threaded with nimble feet,
Dance sedately : face to face they gaze,
Their eyes shining, grave with a perfect pleasure.

W. L. BINYON.

NOCTURN

NDER a stagnant sky,
    Gloom out of gloom uncoiling into gloom,
    The River, jaded and forlorn,
    Welters and wanders wearily—wretchedly on
Yet in and out among the ribs
Of the old skeleton bridge, as in the piles
Of some dead lake-built city, full of skulls
Worm-worn, rat-riddled, mouldy with memories,
Lingers to babble to a broken tune
(Once, O the unvoiced music of my heart!)
So melancholy a soliloquy,
It sounds as it might tell
The secret of the unending grief-in-grain,
The terror of Time and Change and Death,
That wastes this floating transitory world.

What of the incantation
That forced the huddled shapes on yonder shore
To take and wear the night
Like a material majesty?
That touched the shafts of wavering fire
About this miserable welter and wash—
(River, O River of Journeys, River of Dreams!)—
Into long, shining signals from the panes
Of an enchanted pleasure-house
Where life and light might live life lost in life
For ever and evermore?

O Death! O Change! O Time!
Without you, O the insufferable eyes
Of these poor Might-have-beens,
These fatuous, ineffectual Yesterdays!

                                W. E. HENLEY.

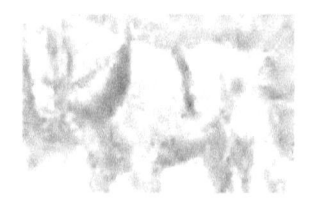

IN WESTMINSTER

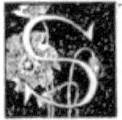T. Margaret's bells,
    Quiring their innocent, old-world canticles,
    Sing in the storied air
    All rosy and golden as with memories
    Of woods at even-song, and sands and seas
Disconsolate for that the night is nigh.
O the low, lingering lights! The large last gleam
(Hark! how the brazen choristers cry and call!)
Touching these solemn ancientries, and there,
The silent River ranging tide-mark high,
The gray-faced Hospital,
With the strange glimmer and glamour of a dream!
The Sabbath peace is in the slumb'rous trees,
And from the wistful, the fast-widowing sky
(Hark! how those plangent comforters call and cry!)
Falls, as in August plots late rose-leaves fall.
The sober Sabbath stir—
Leisurely voices, desultory feet!—
Comes from the dry, dust-coloured street,
Where in their summer frocks the girls go by,
And sweethearts lean and loiter and confer,
Just as they did a hundred years ago,
Just as a hundred years to come they will:
When you and I, Dear Love, lie lost and low,
And sweet-throats none our welkin shall fill
Nor any sunset fade serene and slow;
But, being dead, we shall not grieve to die.

                                      W. E. Hen

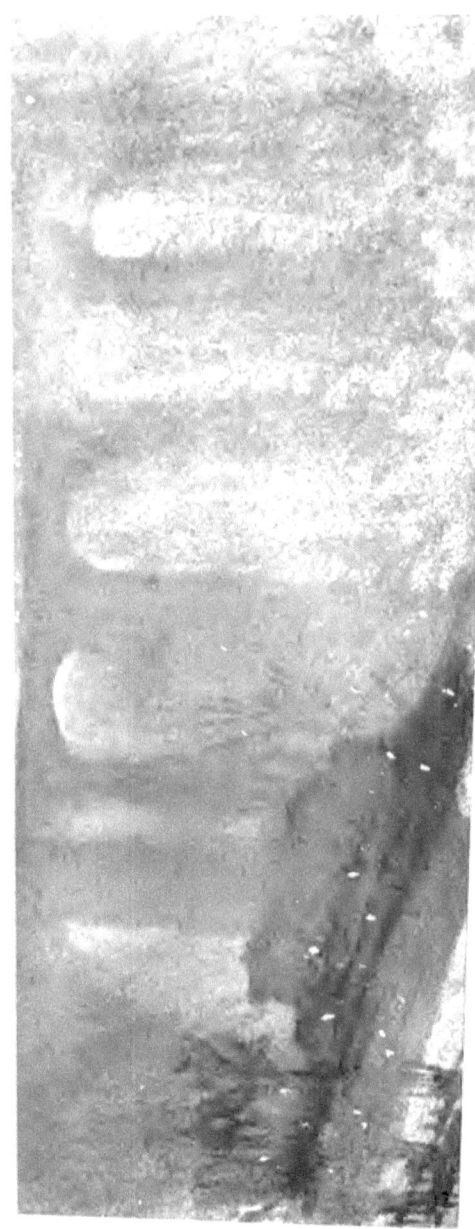

FOG

UT of the poisonous East,
Over a continent of blight,
Like a maleficent Influence released
From the most squalid cellarage of hell,
The Wind-Fiend, the abominable—
The hangman wind that tortures temper and light—
Comes slouching, sullen and obscene,
Hard on the skirts of the embittered night :
And in a cloud unclean
Of excremental humours, roused to strife
By the operation of some ruinous change
Wherever his evil mandate run and range
Into a dire intensity of life,
A craftsman at his bench, he settles down
To the grim job of throttling London Town.

And, by a jealous lightlessness beset
That might have oppressed the dragons of old-time
Crunching and groping in the abysmal slime,
A cave of cut-throat thoughts and villainous dreams,
Hag-rid and crying with cold and dirt and wet,
The afflicted city, prone from mark to mark
In shameful occultation, seems
A nightmare labyrinthine, dim and drifting,
With wavering gulfs and antic heights and shifting
Rent in the stuff of a material dark
Wherein the lamplight, scattered and sick and pale,
Shows like the leper's living blotch of bale :
Uncoiling monstrous into street on street

A LONDON GARLAND

Paven with perils, teeming with mischance,
Where man and beast go blindfold and in dread,
Working with oaths and threats and faltering feet
Somewhither in the hideousness ahead ;
Working through wicked airs and deadly dews
That make the laden robber grin askance
At the good places in his black romance,
And the poor, loitering harlot rather choose
Go pinched and pined to bed
Than lurk and shiver and curse her wretched way
From arch to arch, scouting some threepenny prey.

Forgot his dawns and far-flushed afterglows,
His green garlands and windy eyots forgot,
The old Father-River flows,
His watchfires cores of menace in the gloom,
As he came oozing from the Pit, and bore,
Sunk in his filthily transfigured sides,
Shoals of dishonoured dead to tumble and rot
In the squalor of the universal shore :
His voices sounding through the gruesome air
As from the ferry where the Boat of Doom
With her blaspheming cargo reels and rides :
The while his children, the brave ships,
No more adventurous and fair,
Nor tripping it light of heel as home-bound brides,
But infamously enchanted,
Huddle together in the foul eclipse,
Or feel their course by inches desperately,
As through a tangle of alleys murder-haunted,
From sinister reach to reach out—out—to sea.

And Death the while—
Death with his well-worn, lean, professional smile,
Death in his threadbare working trim—
Comes to your bedside, unannounced and bland,
And with expert, inevitable hand
Feels at your windpipe, fingers you in the lung,
Or flicks the clot well into the labouring heart :
Thus signifying unto old and young,
However hard of mouth or wild of whim,
'Tis time—'tis time by his ancient watch—to part
With books and women and talk and drink and art :
And you go humbly after him

A LONDON GARLAND

To a mean suburban lodging : on the way
To what or where
Not Death, who is old and very wise, can say :
And you—how should you care
So long as, unreclaimed of hell,
The Wind-Fiend, the insufferable,
Thus vicious and thus patient sits him down
To the black job of burking London Town?

W. E. HEN

www.ingramcontent.com/pod-product-compliance
Lightning Source LLC
Chambersburg PA
CBHW021822230426
43669CB00008B/832